"I have worked with this curriculum for more than a decade. I have seen the Spirit of God use this material to lead to the kind of spiritual reflection that encourages spiritual growth and draws one closer to God. I am certain it will be a spiritual catalyst for your group."

—DARRELL BOCK
research professor of New Testament Studies, professor of Spiritual Development and Culture, Dallas Theological Seminary

"The TRANSFORMING LIFE series involves spiritual formation elements that are individual and community-based, reflective and active—all working together in their proper time and manner. It is both scriptural and reality-based in unique and life-changing ways."

—BRAD SMITH
president, Bakke Graduate University

"An outstanding tool in the development of men and women of faith! I have personally used the principles and concepts of the earlier versions of this material for the past eight years; I can assure you that it is a time-tested, invaluable resource that I look forward to using in the years to come."

—DAN BOSCO
community life pastor, Vail Bible Church, Avon, Colorado

IDENTITY

Investigating Who I Am

Center for Christian Leadership at Dallas Theological Seminary

NAVPRESS®

BRINGING TRUTH TO LIFE

The Navigators is an international Christian organization. Our mission is to reach, disciple, and equip people to know Christ and to make Him known through successive generations. We envision multitudes of diverse people in the United States and every other nation who have a passionate love for Christ, live a lifestyle of sharing Christ's love, and multiply spiritual laborers among those without Christ.

NavPress is the publishing ministry of The Navigators. NavPress publications help believers learn biblical truth and apply what they learn to their lives and ministries. Our mission is to stimulate spiritual formation among our readers.

© 2004 by Center for Christian Leadership

ISBN 1-57683-558-8

Cover design by Arvid Wallen
Creative Team: Jay Howver, Karen Lee-Thorp, Cara Iverson, Glynese Northam

Some of the anecdotal illustrations in this book are true to life and are included with the permission of the persons involved. All other illustrations are composites of real situations, and any resemblance to people living or dead is coincidental.

Unless otherwise identified, all Scripture quotations in this publication are taken from the HOLY BIBLE: NEW INTERNATIONAL VERSION® (NIV®). Copyright © 1973, 1978, 1984 by International Bible Society. Used by permission of Zondervan Publishing House. All rights reserved. Other versions include: the New English Translation (NET). Copyright © 2001 by Biblical Studies Press, L.L.C. www.netbible.com. All rights reserved.

Printed in Canada

1 2 3 4 5 6 7 8 9 10 / 08 07 06 05 04

Table of Contents

Acknowledgments

The TRANSFORMING LIFE series is based on a curriculum developed at Dallas Theological Seminary for its Spiritual Formation program, under the guidance of the Center for Christian Leadership. Hundreds of seminary students have benefited from this material, and now this adapted version makes it available to local churches and ministries.

This series would not have been possible without the contributions of many people and the support of Dallas Theological Seminary. The person primarily responsible for this series is Erik Petrik, senior pastor at Vail Bible Church in Vail, Colorado. As the director of the Spiritual Formation program in the late 1990s through 2000, Erik and his team developed the philosophy of this series and its fundamental components. The team he gathered included men and women with great spiritual insight and extensive ministry experience. It was primarily due to Erik's vision and the team's refining, researching, and writing that this series came to life.

In addition, the following persons made significant contributions: Terry Boyle, Barry Jones, Tim Lundy, Tom Miller, Elizabeth Nash, Jim Neathery, Kim Poupart, Kari Stainback, Troy Stringfield, and Monty Waldron. It was my great pleasure to work with each of them and experience the image of Christ in them.

Others who shaped the Spiritual Formation program at Dallas Seminary from the early 1990s are John Contoveros, Pete Deison, Martin Hironaga, David Kanne, Dr. Bill Lawrence, Brad Smith, and David Ward. Special appreciation goes to Pete Deison and David Kanne for their early contribution to what eventually became *Life Story,* and to Dr. Bill Lawrence, who gave the team the freedom to "think outside the box" when he was the executive director of the Center for Christian Leadership. Dr. Andrew Seidel, the current acting executive director, has continued to provide needed support through the process of revising the series for use in churches and ministries. Kerri Gupta contributed much time and energy cleaning up the manuscript. Thanks to her for her editing work.

Dallas Theological Seminary provided the context and the resources necessary for this series. Many students have given valuable feedback in the development at various stages. The support of the seminary administration has been invaluable. This series could not have come into being without its support.

WILLIAM G. MILLER
Resource Development Coordinator
Center for Christian Leadership
Dallas Theological Seminary

A Model of Spiritual Transformation

What's the first thing that comes to mind when you think of spiritual growth? Some picture a solitary individual meditating or praying. While that concept accurately portrays one aspect of Christian spirituality, it doesn't tell the whole story.

Three Aspects of Transformation

The issue of spiritual transformation is not new in the Christian faith. It has been a primary issue, though perhaps given different labels, throughout church history. From the time the Spirit of God descended upon the believers in Jerusalem, God has been transforming the souls of individual believers in the context of local Christian communities.

Preaching has never been and never will be the only element needed for the transformation of Christians into Christ's image. Nor are small-group Bible studies, personal Bible study, Sunday school classes, or even one-on-one discipleship sufficient for growing Christians when they focus solely on communicating biblical information. Therefore, a movement has grown that emphasizes transformation of the believer's inner and outer life and not just transformation of the intellect. Three broad approaches to spiritual transformation have developed.

Fellowship Model

One approach is to create fellowship opportunities. Churches develop structured settings for members to build relationships with others. They may launch small groups that meet in homes. They may convert their Sunday school classes into times of social engagement. These groups enable believers to be intimately involved in one another's lives. The fellowship model focuses on corporate prayer for one another, growth of interpersonal intimacy, and support for each other in times of need. This approach effectively connects believers within a church body.

Spiritual Disciplines Model

A second approach emphasizes disciplines such as meditation, prayer, fasting, and solitude. Such writers as Dallas Willard and Richard Foster have done excellent work on spiritual disciplines. This approach takes seriously the inner life and intimacy with God. However, when used in isolation, this approach can make people think spiritual transformation is a private matter. Even though the spiritual disciplines include communal elements (worship, service, and fellowship), some people treat the private exercises (silent retreats, journaling, meditating on Scripture, prayer, and fasting) as primary. That's a mistake.

Counseling Model

The third approach relies heavily on personal introspection. Christian counseling emphasizes areas of surrounding sin or personal character flaws that cause interpersonal problems or destructive behavior. Counseling seeks to understand the roots of such problems by looking at one's heritage and temperament. Usually in one-on-one interaction, the counselor probes for the root issues hidden beneath the surface problem. Discovering these deeper issues can shed light on a person's consistent failure to make wise choices. This approach focuses on identifying and dealing with those internal obstacles that prevent spiritual growth. Dealing with the issues is a key component in spiritual transformation.

The TRANSFORMING LIFE Model — An Integrated Approach

The three approaches are all valuable, but when taken alone they each have weaknesses. The fellowship model can fail to guide believers toward growth. The spiritual disciplines model can neglect to emphasize authentic and intimate Christian community, which is necessary for growth. The counseling model can fail to value the role that spiritual disciplines can have in growth. It also risks focusing on deficiencies so much that the person never benefits from the resources of God's grace. It can focus too intently upon the person's sin and failure and not enough on God's enabling power toward growth in holiness.

Therefore, TRANSFORMING LIFE brings in elements from all three approaches. The series tries to balance the inward and outward elements of spiritual transformation. Its theme is:

> Experiencing divine power through relationships;
> Striving together toward maturity in Christ.

We believe a particular context is essential to the transformation process. That context is authentic community in which people come to trust each other. Though one-on-one relationships can be effective, we believe that multiple relationships are more effective. While one individual can spur another toward growth, that one individual has limited gifts and abilities. Also, though we value the spiritual disciplines, we see them as means toward the end of complete transformation of the believer's inner and outer life. Disciplines aren't ends in themselves. Finally, we think believers need to seek greater understanding of sin's dynamic in their lives. They need to see potential blind spots or obstacles to their spiritual well-being and learn to deal with the root issues beneath their areas of struggle.

Our working definition of the Christian's transformation is:

> The process by which God forms Christ's character in believers by the ministry of the Spirit, in the context of community, and in accordance with biblical standards. This process involves the transformation of the whole person in thoughts, behaviors, and styles of relating with God and others. It results in a life of service to others and witness for Christ.

While the transformation process is an end in itself, the ultimate end is Christ's glory. He is the One adored by those who experience His presence and are transformed by Him. They, in turn, seek to exalt Him in the world.

Because each person is unique, God's formative process is unique for each. And though the Spirit of God is the One who transforms souls, each individual has personal responsibility in the process. Many spiritual disciplines can contribute, yet God is primarily concerned with transforming the whole person, not just patterns of behavior. For this reason, no one method (be it a traditional spiritual discipline or another method) is the single critical component.

A well-rounded experience of activities is the greatest catalyst for growth. For example, providing for the needy helps us better understand and participate in Christ's love for the outcast, needy, lonely, and depressed. A small group offers the chance to encourage a struggling believer, learn from others how to apply God's Word personally, and comfort someone in his or her grief. A regular time for prayer can help us reflect upon God's intimate love, remember personal needs and the needs of others as they are brought before God, release anxieties to God, and express dependence upon God. Spiritual transformation occurs neither exclusively in private nor exclusively in public. For the character of Christ to be developed most fully, believers need an inner, private intimacy with God; an active, working love for others; and a pursuit of Christlike integrity.

TRANSFORMING LIFE depends solely on peer leadership. Groups don't need to be led by trained ministers. Leaders are more like facilitators—they don't need to have all the answers because group members learn from each other. The leader's role is to create an environment that fosters growth and encouragement.

Still, all small-group ministries need consistent coaching for the lay leaders. The group leaders need ministers and pastors to train and encourage them. A small-group ministry will raise all sorts of issues for leaders to deal with as people become honest about their lives in a trusting community. A group leader may need guidance about how to respond to a group member who shares that he has been having an e-mail "affair" and has not told his wife. Another leader may feel discouraged when group members drop out. Still another may wonder how to deal with two group members who are consistently angry with each other. It's important to provide support to those who take the risk to develop such an authentic environment for growth.

The Four Themes of This Series

Instead of aiming for competency in a set of skills or techniques, this series helps people identify the areas that must be developed in a believer's life. In other words, while it's necessary for a believer to know the "how-tos" of the Christian life, it's not sufficient. Knowing how to do personal Bible study and being good at sharing Christ with others are praiseworthy skills. Developing these skills, however, is not the end goal but the means by which we live out who we are as new creatures in Christ. That's why this series addresses four critical components of the Christian life: identity, community, integrity, and ministry.

This series proposes that the Christian life involves:

> knowing your identity in Christ
> *so that*
> you can make yourself known to others in a Christian community
> *so that*
> you can pursue a lifetime of growth in the context of community
> *so that*
> you are best equipped to glorify Christ by serving others.

Identity

To understand our need for transformation, we must understand who we are currently, both as individuals and as members of the body of Christ. Who we are has undoubtedly been shaped by our past. Therefore, we explore various aspects of our identity, such as our heritage and temperament. What do these tell us about who we are and what we value? The interaction during this study bonds us and builds trust among us. Our goal is not to analyze, criticize, or control each other but is to grow and affirm what God is doing in and through one another.

In *Identity*, we ultimately want group members to see themselves in light of their identity in Christ. However, many of the values we actually live out stem from such influences as temperament, family background, and culture. Not all of those values are contrary to our new identity in Christ. For example, the value one person places on honesty, which he learned from his parents, is affirmed by his identity in Christ.

It can take a long time—more than a lifetime allows—for the Spirit of God to transform our values to line up with our new identity in Christ. We cooperate with the Spirit when we reflect on what our values are and how well they line up with our identity in Christ as described in Scripture.

One very significant characteristic of our identity in Christ is that we are part of the body of Christ. The Christian life cannot be lived in isolation.

Community

So, while talking about *my* place in Christ, I need to pay attention to *our* place in Christ as a community. Understanding our corporate identity in

Christ is crucial for a healthy community transformation process. The *Community* study helps a group not only understand how a Christian community develops but also experience a growing sense of community.

In order to experience intimate community in the biblical sense, we must learn to reveal ourselves to others. We need to honestly, freely, and thoughtfully tell our stories. Our modern culture makes it easy for people to live isolated and anonymous lives. Because we and others move frequently, we may feel it's not worth the effort to be vulnerable in short-lived relationships. However, we desperately need to keep intentionally investing in significant relationships.

Real involvement in others' lives requires more than what the term *fellowship* has too often come to mean. Real involvement includes holding certain values in common and practicing a lifestyle we believe is noble, while appreciating that this lifestyle doesn't make us perfect. Rather, this lifestyle is a commitment to let God continue to spiritually form us.

Community includes a group exercise, "Life Story," that has been tremendously effective in building community and enhancing self-understanding. "Life Story" walks a person through the process of putting together a personal, creative presentation of the most formative relationships and experiences of his or her life. As people share their stories with each other, a deep level of trust and commitment grows.

Integrity

By the time a group has experienced *Identity* and *Community* together, members have built significant intimacy and trust. Now they're ready to pursue a harder step. It's the heart of our approach to spiritual transformation. Many believers greatly underestimate the necessity of intimacy and trust for successful growth in Christian holiness. But we must be able to share honestly those areas in which we need transformation. We can deal with deep issues of growth only in a community in which we're deeply known by others. We need others who have our best interests at heart. They must also be people we trust to hold sensitive issues in genuine confidence.

Why does the pursuit of Christian holiness need to occur in community? There are at least two reasons. First, we need accountability in the areas of sin with which we struggle. When we confess our struggles to a group, we become accountable to all of the members to press on toward growth. Because the group is aware of our sin, we can't hide it in darkness, where it retains a hold on our life and can make crippling guilt a permanent fixture in our walk. If we're struggling, we have not one but several people to lean on. In addition, the corporate, or group, setting increases the likelihood of support from someone else who has struggled in the same way. In one-on-one accountability, one person may not be able to relate well to the other's struggles. He or she may have different areas of struggle.

The second benefit of corporate pursuit of holiness is that without the encouragement and stimulus of other Christians, we're often blind to the ways in which we need to grow. In the counsel of many who care for us, there can be greater wisdom. If some believers are blind to being hospitable, the hospitality of another believer can spur them on to develop that quality in their own lives. If some never think about how to speak encouraging words, the encouraging speech of another can become contagious.

Ministry

With *Identity*, *Community*, and *Integrity* as a foundation, believers are prepared to discern how God wants them to serve in the body of Christ. "Where can I serve?" is not an optional question; every believer should ask it. Nor is this a matter simply for individual reflection. Rather, we can best discern where and how to serve while in community with people who know our past, interests, struggles, and talents. The community can affirm what they see in us and may know of opportunities to serve that we're unaware of.

How many terrific musicians are sitting in pews every Sunday because they lack the confidence to volunteer? Those gifted people might merely need others who know them well to encourage them to serve. Maybe someone's life story revealed that while growing up she played in a band. Someone might ask, "What have you done with that interest lately?"

The Layout of *Identity*

Each of the ten sessions has the following features:
- *Session Aims* states a goal for you as an individual and one for the group.
- *Preparation* tells what assignment(s) you need to complete ahead of

time in order to get the most out of the group. For this study, much of the preparation will involve completing "Life Inventory" exercises. The "Life Inventory" exercises can be found on pages 89-120.

- Some sessions include a biblical exercise. A biblical exercise is a self-study in which you'll spend time outside the group studying a passage from Scripture.
- *Introduction* sets up the session's topic.
- *Content* provides material around which group discussions and exercises will focus. You should read the "Introduction" and "Content" sections before your group meeting so you'll be prepared to discuss them.
- *Conclusion* wraps up the session and sets the scene for the next one.
- *Assignment* lists "homework" to complete before the next session meeting.

In this way, each session includes all three aspects of transformation: personal introspection, spiritual disciplines, and the experience of God in relationships. Through all of these means, the Spirit of God will be at work in your life.

A Method for the Biblical Exercises

The biblical exercises will guide you through a self-study of a passage that relates to the session topic. You'll begin by making observations about the passage. Pay attention to the following categories:

Who?

Identify persons in the passage: the descriptions of persons, the relationships between persons, and the conditions of persons.

What?

Identify subjects in the passage: the issues or topics being addressed.

When?

Identify time in the passage: duration of time that passes and when the events occurred in relationship to one another.

Where?

Identify places in the passage: the descriptions of locations, the relationships of places to other places, and the relationships of persons to the places.

Why?

Identify purposes in the passage: the expressions of purpose by the author and/or the characters.

How?

Identify events in the passage: the descriptions of events unfolding, the relationships between events, and the order of events.

In *Living By the Book*, Dr. Howard Hendricks and William Hendricks identify six categories that aid the process of observation. They encourage readers to "look for things that are (1) emphasized, (2) repeated, (3) related, (4) alike, (5) unalike, or (6) true to life."[1]

After you make observations, you will interpret the passage. Interpretation involves determining what the main point of the passage is. Then you'll reflect on how the main point applies to your life. Be sure to ask for God's guidance in your reflection. After all, the purpose of Scripture is for God to speak to us and, as a result, for our lives to be transformed.

Human Nature

What makes someone human? This question starts us on the journey toward understanding our identity in Christ. We are called to Christ as human beings, so we must understand the fundamental purpose of human beings. This session explores God's purpose in creating humankind. What binds us all together?

In future sessions, we'll discuss aspects of our identity that are "earthly." Our earthly identity includes those traits that all of humankind—both believers and nonbelievers—possess. After that, we'll examine aspects of our identity that are entirely "heavenly"—characteristics we have because we've trusted in Christ.

For now, though, what do we share in common as human beings?

Session Aims

Individual Aim: To identify universal characteristics of human nature from chapters 1–2 of the book of Genesis.

Group Aim: To gain a greater understanding of human nature and its effects on human experiences.

Preparation

Complete *Biblical Exercise: Genesis 1–2* beginning on page 20.

Read *Session 1: Human Nature.*

Biblical Exercise: Genesis 1–2

Read the first two chapters of Genesis. Also, read "A Method for the
Biblical Exercises" beginning on page 17.

Observation — "What Do I See?"

1. Who are the persons (including God) in the passage? What is the condition of those persons?

   — Adam - created Dominle
     eve -
     God -

2. What are they saying or doing? (Look especially for statements or actions that are emphasized, repeated, related, alike, unalike, or true to life.)
   God Creaty - Given /over his regos. hiy
                          good each time..
   Adam — Name all animals.
     Eve

3. When did this take place?
   — In the begssing.
   → 10~15 k.

4. Where did this take place?

  — Rivers Planet Garden of Eden.

5. Why did it happen?

  — God was bored.

- What changed between the beginning and the end of chapter 1?

  — Creation

- What changed between the beginning and the end of chapter 2?

  — None   Garden of Eden   aswell

Interpretation Phase 1 — "What Did It Mean Then?"

1. Coming to Terms — Are there any words in the passage that you don't understand? Write down anything you found confusing about the passage.

2. Finding Where It Fits—What clues does the Bible give about the meaning of this passage?

- Immediate Context (the passage being studied)

  - *What God Creat*
  - *God Did Geah*

- Remote Context (passages that come before and after the one being studied)

  - *Good*
  - *Marrige*

3. Getting into Their Sandals—An Exercise in Imagination (Focus on Genesis 2 for this exercise.)

- How did it look?

  Huse Jungle.

- How did it sound?

  -Big.

- How did it smell?

  -Flowers.

- How did it feel?

  - 75.

- How did it taste?

  Fruit voes good.

Interpretation Phase 2 — **"What Does It Mean Now?"**

1. What is the timeless truth in the passage? In one or two sentences, write down what you learned about God from Genesis 1–2.

—Intended all For Maed Mad in his Image
—Gave us free will.
— Manage this

2. How does that truth work today?

—Corrupt.
—

Application — **"What Can I Do to Make This Truth Real?"**

1. What can I do to make this truth real for myself?

→ free will.
— No Nuke.

2. For my family?

3. For my friends?

4. For the people who live near me?

5. For the rest of the world?

Introduction

"What am I doing here?" For those who believe in the one God of the Bible, the answer is found in the book of Genesis. Its first two chapters describe how God made humans and their world. Debates about the process by which God made the universe can become heated. However, the main topic of the chapters is God's purpose in creating the world. The central figures are God and the human species. What we want to focus on in this session is the fundamental purpose of human beings. This session is not intended to address evolutionism and creationism. Rather, it centers on identifying God's purpose for creating humankind.

Content

Genesis 1 describes creation in a pattern involving two purposes: ruling and multiplying. God created the sun, moon, and stars to rule impersonally over the earth. He created the animals to multiply on the earth. Humans, however, were created to both multiply and rule over creation. Obviously, our form of ruling over the earth is different from that of the sun, moon, and stars. Genesis 2 further explains that distinction by narrowing the lens to the creation of Adam and Eve.

This chapter adds a new element to the creation of humans: relationship. The heavenly bodies rule over the earth without personal relationships.

They have no sense of personhood. However, God gives to humankind the capacity of relationship, both with the Creator and with one another. Relationship involves the abilities to reason and to communicate through language.

After making these observations, we must interpret the passage's meaning. First, from God's actions in these chapters, what do we learn about Him?
- God is a God of order. (Creation is a process.)
- God is eternal. (As Creator He preexists all that is created.)
- God is omnipotent (all-powerful).
- God is sovereign. (He holds absolute authority.)
- God is relational. (He created humans to be in relationship with Him and with each other.)
- God creates with purpose (sun and moon to rule, birds and fish to multiply, mankind to multiply and rule).
- God alone is God—there is no other. (He is the Creator; no other god precedes Him.)

Next, what do we learn about ourselves?
- We are significant (made by God, made in His image, highest of earthly creatures).
- We are created to rule the earth, not to be ruled by it. (We have work to do; we have purpose; we have responsibility.)
- We were created to be dependent upon the earth (given plants to eat).
- We are dependent upon God. (He gave us life; He gives us food to stay alive.)

What are the implications for us? First, every human has a broad purpose from the Creator God. We all share this universal aspect of our identity: We are to multiply and rule relationally. God intentionally created Adam with a relational nature. God saw Adam alone and said, "It is not good" (Genesis 2:18). Because we all share this relational nature, we must be designed to work together. Each person was not given his or her own "earth" to govern. Instead, we are all designed to rule, but to rule together as peers. No human has a right to rule in an absolute manner over any other. Hierarchy among human beings may be necessary for a purpose and even ordained by God in a particular context (such as parental authority over children and governing officials over citizens), but there is no indication in Genesis or elsewhere that one person has absolute authority over another. There is no class of humans that is above or below the others.

Second, God is in the business of bringing order out of chaos. From the formless mass He created an ordered universe. Likewise, part of the image of God in us is to bring order out of chaos. Rulers make judgments about what should be done. They choose between options on moral bases. The heavenly bodies are animated by fixed laws of nature. But humans are able to make choices based on moral judgment. They are not completely at the mercy of their environment but can order and change their environment.

Third, God made "male" and "female" in His own image. Humans were created to be an image or visible expression of God's nature. Obviously, God's image in humankind is limited. It's not a replication of Him, like some sort of clone. Rather, men and women were created to display on earth a physically present image of its Creator. And because both Adam and Eve were created with this image, it's clear that men and women both were designed to glorify their Creator.

So we see three aspects of human nature:
- Humankind was created to have a shared purpose of ruling over the earth in cooperation with one another and mutual submission to God's authority (see Genesis 1:26-28).
- Humankind was created to order our own lives and the earth in accordance with moral imperatives (see Genesis 2:15-17). God designed humans to live in obedience to His commands.
- Humankind was created to reflect the Creator's nature and glory (see Genesis 1:27; Exodus 34:29-35).

Conclusion

Human identity is grounded in God's design: We are to be mutually submissive to God's authority, rule over our lives and the earth with moral judgment, and display His image to the physical world. This insight gives Christians a distinctive view of the dignity of all human beings. Regardless of our circumstances, our lives have purpose. Our purpose depends not on *what* we do (for instance, our jobs) but on *how* we do what we do, as we will see in "Session 2: Roles."

Assignment

Read *Session 2: Roles.*

Read *Life Inventory: Introduction* on page 89.

Complete the *Life Inventory: Roles* exercise beginning on page 91.

Roles

"Who am I?" This question goes beyond the question asked at the beginning of session 1. It doesn't ask who human beings are corporately but rather who each of us is as an individual. Though a simple question, it often leads to myriad complex answers. And despite its importance, many of us have never taken the time to answer it.

Many people assume that we know who we are. Some may have the attitude that life is better spent in action than in reflection. After all, if I'm a salesperson, I need to focus primarily on making sales. If I'm an avid mountain biker, I will make time to go on as many rides as I can. However, such descriptions miss the mark. Understanding your identity in such terms can blind you to God's design in your life.

The assumption that most people have a handle on who they are currently and how they need to grow and change in the future is incorrect. "Who am I?" We begin to answer this question by exploring the relationship between our identity and our roles.

Session Aims

Individual Aim: To identify individual roles and their relationship to your identity.

Group Aim: To discuss the relationship between identity and roles and to begin to distinguish between the two.

Preparation

Read *Session 2: Roles*.

Read *Life Inventory: Introduction* on page 89.

Complete the *Life Inventory: Roles* exercise beginning on page 91.

Introduction

> *The wisdom of the prudent is to give thought to their ways, but the folly of fools is deception. (Proverbs 14:8)*

Content

Life in twenty-first-century America is transient. Job changes and relocations uproot people from home, church, and even family and friends. Changes of this magnitude disrupt and change one's sense of identity.

It's challenging enough to find our way around a new town—locating grocery stores, figuring out what auto mechanic we can trust, and discovering the fun recreation spots. But the real challenge of moving is establishing an entirely new set of relationships. For some period of time, we lack community. We neither know nor are known by others.

We may begin to question who we are and how others perceive us. We may feel destabilized and vulnerable. But even an identity crisis can be a blessing. There's no better time to evaluate our identity than when we are forced to see ourselves in a new light.

Consider some times of transition from your own life, such as moving to a new city. Did you wrestle with your identity? How often during that time were you asked questions such as "Where do you work?" or "Where are you from?" These questions are often attempts to ask the fundamental question "Who are you?"

Often, our first response to such questions is to list our various roles. Depending upon how the questions are asked, we might describe the roles we have at our workplace ("I'm an accountant"), in our home ("I have three kids"), or in our hobbies ("I play on a softball team").

On the surface we may feel we fully understand our identity when we list all of our roles. Though we may find great significance and even stability in the roles we fulfill, can we say they completely encompass our identity? For example, can someone describe who he or she truly is by stating, "I'm a buyer for a retail company, I'm the mother of two teenage daughters, and I am an active member of the PTA"? If that were the case, our identity would undergo a major transition every time we made a life change.

While describing roles may be how we attempt to reveal our identity, those roles don't truly encompass who we are. It's better to seek our identity in *how* we perform our roles.

For instance, the following are statements of roles (*what* a person does):
- I am an engineer.
- I am a hospital volunteer.
- I am a mother of three.

By contrast, the following statements tell *how* a person lives out his or her roles:
- I am trustworthy.
- I am reserved.
- I am ambitious.

These statements are much more useful indicators of identity. They remain more stable when the person leaves his or her engineering job or when his or her children grow up and leave home.

Your roles are the interface between you and the world around you. The way a man fathers his kids demonstrates core aspects of his identity. Is he gentle, or harsh? Is he actively involved, or distant? How a waitress performs her responsibilities reveals a part of who she is. Is she courteous, or rude? Is she hardworking, or lazy? Observing patterns in the way people live out their roles gives insight into their identity.

> You are not what you do,
> but how you do what you do
> reveals who you are.

Thinking of your roles like this may be a new concept for you. When you begin to view your identity in these terms, it can be difficult to get a handle on it. The rest of this study will help you gain clarity.

Conclusion

Evaluating our identity is a difficult and sometimes confusing process. Though our identity affects the way we live out our roles, our identity and our roles are not one and the same. Roles are based on our present circumstances. Certain aspects of our identity develop over time, whereas others are "given" as part of God's design. Gender is one of those aspects. We will discuss that issue in session 3.

Assignment

Read *Session 3: Gender.*

Complete the *Life Inventory: Gender* exercise beginning on page 94.

Gender

Session 2 introduced the distinction between role and identity. We usually express roles in statements about what we do ("I am an engineer"), while identity statements express who we are, regardless of what we do ("I am trustworthy"). The attributes of identity, what sort of person we are, will go with each of us into whatever roles we fill and will transform the ways we carry out any given role.

We must grasp this distinction as we move into the discussion of gender. Gender is one key component of identity. Being a man or being a woman affects our outlook on life in ways we may be unaware of. In this session we will ask, "What kind of man or woman am I?" and "Where and from whom did I learn to be that kind of man or woman?"

Session Aims

Individual Aim: To explore past influences and present views regarding gender.

Group Aim: To gain greater understanding of the influence of gender on how people think and act.

Preparation

Read *Session 3: Gender*.

Complete the *Life Inventory: Gender* exercise beginning on page 94.

Introduction

While our biological sex traits (anatomy and physiology) are determined at birth, our sense of what it means to be male or female, masculine or feminine, develops through our family, culture, and experiences. One striking example in Scripture that points to the difference between men and women is when God gives distinct curses to Adam and Eve after they eat the forbidden fruit:

> *To the woman he said,*
>
> *"I will greatly increase your pains in*
>   *childbearing;*
>   *with pain you will give birth to children.*
> *Your desire will be for your husband,*
>   *and he will rule over you."*
>
> *To Adam he said, "Because you listened to your wife and ate from the tree about which I commanded you, 'You must not eat of it,'*
>
> *"Cursed is the ground because of you;*
>   *through painful toil you will eat of it*
>   *all the days of your life.*
> *It will produce thorns and thistles for you,*
>   *and you will eat the plants of the field.*
> *By the sweat of your brow*
>   *you will eat your food*
> *until you return to the ground,*
>   *since from it you were taken;*
> *for dust you are*
>   *and to dust you will return." (Genesis 3:16-19)*

Content

A proper understanding of sexuality and gender must be based on Scripture. While it's not within the scope of this study to give a complete overview, we'll flesh out a few fundamental ideas.

First, men and women are equal as God's representatives:

> *In the Lord, however, woman is not independent of man, nor is man independent of woman. For as woman came from man, so also man is born of woman. But everything comes from God. (1 Corinthians 11:11-12)*

Scripture never portrays either men or women as superior to the other in foundational issues, such as one's potential to glorify God.

The Creation account provides the bedrock for understanding gender issues throughout Scripture:

> *So God created man in his own image,*
>   *in the image of God he created him;*
> *male and female He created them. (Genesis 1:27)*

Raymond Ortlund Jr., pastor and former professor at Trinity Evangelical Divinity School, notes the distinct emphasis in each line:

> Line one asserts the divine creation of man. We came from God. Line two overlaps with line one, except that it highlights the divine image in man. We bear a resemblance to God. Line three boldly affirms the dual sexuality of man. We are male and female.[1]

This passage in Genesis demonstrates that each human being reflects God's image. Humankind is the image bearer, and humankind is male and female. As the Creation account continues, both man and woman are commissioned to rule and fill the earth. The command in 1:28 is for humans to "be fruitful and increase in number; fill the earth and subdue it." Humanity has the responsibility to produce life, both spiritual and physical.

Likewise, God commissioned humanity to rule over His creation. Ortlund continues, "Man was created as royalty in God's world, male and female alike bearing the divine glory equally."[2]

But the equality of men and women does not diminish the differences between them. The Creation account of Genesis 2 provides insight into these differences. "Then the LORD God said, 'It is not good for the man to be alone. I will make him a helper suitable for him'" (verse 18). The only part of Creation that God judged as not good was that the first man was alone. But God did not simply create another male human. Adam, representing all maleness, was insufficient to carry out the mandate to fill and subdue the earth apart from the creation of femaleness found in Eve.

Old Testament scholar Allen Ross points out that "helper" (Hebrew: *ezer*) is not a demeaning term:

God is usually the one described as the "helper" (Exod. 18:4; Deut. 33:7; 1 Sam. 7:12; Ps. 20:2; 46:1). The word essentially describes one who provides what is lacking in the man, who can do what the man alone cannot do. . . . The man was thus created in such a way that he needs the help of a partner. Or we may say that human beings cannot fulfill their destiny except in mutual assistance.[3]

Ross continues by explaining the concept of a "suitable" helper:

The man and the woman thus correspond physically, socially, and spiritually . . . the woman by relative difference but essential equality would be man's fitting complement. What he lacked ("not good") she supplied; and it would be safe to say that what she lacked, he supplied, for life in common requires mutual help.[4]

We can't overlook the male/female equality before God. Both in personal relationship with God as our Father and in our ability to fulfill the divine mandate for humanity, men and women are equal. But as Ortlund notes, this equality "does not constitute an undifferentiated sameness." He expands:

The very fact that God created human beings in the dual modality of male and female cautions us against an unqualified equation of the two sexes. This profound and beautiful distinction, which some belittle as "a matter of mere anatomy," is not a biological triviality or accident. It is God who wants men to be men and women to be women.[5]

What does it mean for men to be men and women to be women? If God made us with differences that are complementary to fulfill the divine commission, how should those differences be expressed?

We would have no problem understanding and living in a truly complementary manner if sin had not entered the world. Sin has devastated interpersonal relationships. God's judgments in Genesis 3 show how sin has affected the male/female relationship.

In the judgment on Eve in verse 16, God says, "Your desire will be for your husband, and he will rule over you." The term *desire* in this verse is similar to the usage in Genesis 4:7, where sin desires Cain. It means a prompting for evil. Likewise, the term *rule* in this verse refers to dominion or mastery. The punishment would fit the crime. As the woman will desire to usurp, rather than complement, male authority, the man will seek to dominate, rather than honor and respect, his "helper." Ross notes,

> If Eve is an archetype, that is, if she represents every woman as Adam represents every man, then the story portrays a character- istic of human nature—the woman at her worst would be a nemesis to the man, and the man at his worst would dominate the woman.[6]

However, with salvation comes a restoration of all aspects of creation. The restoration of true equality can only be found in Christ.

> *There is neither Jew nor Greek, slave nor free, male nor female, for you are all one in Christ Jesus. If you belong to Christ, then you are Abraham's seed, and heirs according to the promise. (Galatians 3:28-29)*

Likewise, the restoration of the male/female complementary relationship is found in Christ. As believers who desire to reflect God's image and pro- mote God's glory, we must seek to understand what it means to be a Christian man or woman.

Conclusion

Scripture does not clearly define every aspect of gender issues. Even so, we must continue to explore what it means to be a man or woman in Christ. This topic is much debated, but it's worthwhile for each believer to person- ally seek wisdom about how gender influences the way roles are performed.

Assignment

Read *Session 4: Temperament.*

Complete the *Life Inventory: Temperament* exercise beginning on page 98.

Temperament

Like gender, temperament is a component of our "earthly identity." It's part of every person's life. Each of us tends to respond to certain situations in similar ways. We also tend to relate to certain kinds of people in similar ways. These tendencies are at the core of temperament. While temperament is hard to define and assess, it's still valuable to explore because it's shaped by God's sovereign design of our lives.

Session Aims

Individual Aim: To explore your temperament and its impact on your identity.

Group Aim: To better understand group members' temperaments in order to appreciate the impact on their lives.

Preparation

Read *Session 4: Temperament*.

Complete the *Life Inventory: Temperament* exercise beginning on page 98.

Introduction

One way we can get to know God better is to gain a greater appreciation for how He has sovereignly designed us and equipped us to function in His world. The self-assessment you'll do in "Life Inventory" will help you gain greater self-awareness and understand the impact of temperament on your life.

Content

Standardized personal assessments (profiles, tests, and inventories) of temperament are all based on observations found to be generally true about people who have similar attributes. Their strength is that they can provide quick access to helpful (if general) self-knowledge. Their weakness is that while people with similar personality traits have much in common, every person is unique by God's design.

One of the most popular personal assessment tests is the Myers-Briggs Type Indicator. The most helpful way to profit from standardized assessments is to confirm their results with what you know about yourself and with feedback from those who know you well. Thus, while the tests may be useful tools, they don't supersede the Holy Spirit's illumination through God's Word, prayer, and people.

Temperament describes tendencies (patterns in your behavior) that are similar to patterns in the behavior of others. For instance, some people prefer to think out loud when trying to solve a problem. They expect that the solution will become evident through discussion. Other people consider solutions in their own minds, and when they speak, they voice their conclusions. If both kinds of people are working on a project and they are unaware of their different approaches, they often experience conflict. For example, Susan, who thinks out loud, becomes annoyed when Jason criticizes her ideas prematurely. While she's simply trying to work out a solution, he assumes that her comments represent a final proposal for the solution. In contrast, he needs time to work out a solution in his head. Susan becomes frustrated because Jason isn't participating with her in working out a solution.

Consider another example. One company's employees all receive gift certificates at the end of the year. They receive their gifts without any notification or acknowledgment by the administration. In another company, no gift is given, but the president personally goes around to each employee and gives specific examples of why he appreciates his or her work. One person may feel fully appreciated by receiving a gift certificate but wouldn't feel valued by verbal acknowledgment; words without some tangible gift may seem empty. For another person, the gift certificate without any verbal appreciation might raise feelings of disappointment: "They're just trying to buy my loyalty."

Conclusion

Understanding your temperament can make you aware of which of your tendencies to encourage and which ones to avoid. If you know your own preference is gifts over appreciative words, you may need to remind yourself to be grateful when a friend expresses appreciation to you through verbal compliments. Awareness of your own and others' temperaments can greatly enhance your ability to love others well.

Assignment

Read *Session 5: Heritage*.

Complete the *Life Inventory: Heritage* exercise beginning on page 109.

Complete the *Life Inventory: Values I* exercise beginning on page 112.

Heritage

In session 4, we examined how temperament influences our identity. In this session, we'll look at the final component of earthly identity: heritage. We each have a unique personal history that affects how we answer the question "Who am I?" Such factors as when, where, and to whom we were born all affect our answer. Some additional factors include where we grew up, what schools we attended, what traditions we engaged in, and any major transitions we went through. These are all aspects of our heritage that we carry with us today.

Enjoy this opportunity to trace the foundational roots of your life.

Session Aims

Individual Aim: To explore your personal heritage and its impact upon your identity.

Group Aim: To better understand group members' heritages in order to appreciate the impact on their lives.

Preparation

Read *Session 5: Heritage*.

Complete the *Life Inventory: Heritage* exercise beginning on page 109.

Complete the *Life Inventory: Values I* exercise beginning on page 112.

Introduction

heritage: that which comes or belongs to one by reason of birth; an inherited lot or portion[1]

Heritage is the environment into which someone is born and raised. We might think that because we are redeemed in Christ, our heritage shouldn't matter. We might reason that if we are mature in Christ, our heritage should affect our identity very little. There are valid biblical truths behind such thoughts. We are now free from the bondage imposed on us by certain aspects of our heritage. For example, someone raised in a family in which fear was the motive for obedience is now free to respond to God in obedience rather than respond to the fear of men, even though the believer may pay a price for following Christ. Or when loving an enemy results in personal pain or loss, the believer is free to pursue a godly life in spite of what his or her heritage may have taught him or her.

Still, sometimes a person's heritage contains elements that contribute to godly character. For instance, someone raised in a mainstream culture that valued relationships will tend to prioritize people over tasks. In that kind of culture, tasks don't get in the way of valuing people and relationships.

The purpose of this session is not to judge the value of one's heritage but rather to take inventory of it. We take this inventory keeping in mind that our heritage does influence the way we live. Ultimately, we want to explore how to respond to what our heritage has taught us — whether to embrace a given inherited trait as godly or to reject it. However, the first step is to identify characteristics from our heritage so that we can later make accurate judgments.

Content

> *He himself gives all men life and breath and everything else. From one man he made every nation of men, that they should inhabit the whole earth; and he determined the times set for them and the exact places where they should live. (Acts 17:25-26)*

Although we are citizens of a heavenly culture that has its own heavenly identity, we are still living as citizens of this earth. Missiology scholar David Hesselgrave writes, "Though Christianity is supracultural in its origin and truth, it is cultural in its application."[2] We apply Christianity in the midst of identities that have been greatly shaped by our heritage.

This truth affects our ability to communicate the Christian message from one culture to another. When sharing the gospel cross-culturally, we must try to make the message clear and accurate in that particular cultural setting. The same principle applies when we try to live out our faith. Our unique heritage affects the way we try to live out our identity in Christ within our communities.

God's providential hand developed a particular heritage for each person. The story of Joseph illustrates the blessing of seeing God's purpose through the good and the bad of our backgrounds:

> *Then Joseph said to his brothers, "Come close to me." When they had done so, he said, "I am your brother Joseph, the one you sold into Egypt! And now, do not be distressed and do not be angry with yourselves for selling me here, because it was to save lives that God sent me ahead of you. For two years now there has been famine in the land, and for the next five years there will not be plowing and reaping. But God sent me ahead of you to preserve for you a remnant on earth and to save your lives by a great deliverance.*
>
> *"So then, it was not you who sent me here, but God. He made me father to Pharaoh, lord of his entire household and ruler of all Egypt." (Genesis 45:4-8)*

For a special purpose, God used Joseph's unique heritage as a son of Jacob who became an Egyptian civil servant. Although some aspects of our heritage are ungodly and some are godly, God has superintended the entire process and desires to use it uniquely for His glory and our good.

Heritage begins with birth and develops through life circumstances. Although you can state in a few words when, where, and to whom you were born, those facts are more than just data on a page: They have had far-reaching implications in your life.

We'll focus on three cultural categories from which heritage develops: mainstream culture, family culture, and subcultures.

Mainstream Culture

On the broadest level, mainstream culture involves the historical time period in which we've lived. Mainstream culture consists of those characteristics that were realities within the local community where you were born and raised. It might include characteristics of religion (Christian, religious, non-religious, pluralistic), ethnic environment (homogeneous, multicultural, minority in majority culture), political environment (democracy, socialism, conservative, liberal), media (sources of news and entertainment; exposure to radio, TV, and printed materials), traditions (holidays, historical events, dietary habits, fashion), and art (purpose, emphasis on freedom of expression). While the mainstream culture is the larger environment that influenced you, your family culture reveals more specific expressions of each of these categories.

Family Culture

Family culture is the pattern of behaviors and values that individuals learn because of the way their family related and lived out roles. This culture is the one that influences most people to the greatest degree. It's the environment in which most people have spent the most time, especially in their early childhood years. Louis Luzbetak, another missiology scholar, writes,

> An individual to a large extent reflects the values that he or she has *learned* (either through intended education, conscious imitation, or unconscious absorption) from those with whom he or she is in contact. In fact, the closer and the earlier the contact, especially if it is continuous, the greater the impact.[3]

Families develop certain patterns of thinking and behavior. For example, one person's tendency to be aggressive in conflict may stem from the way his or her family typically dealt with it.

Family culture influences some people less than others. As the family unit breaks down, children can become more influenced by the mainstream culture or subcultures.

Subcultures

These are the various environments outside the family culture but distinct from the mainstream culture. An example is the Boy Scouts. For a certain boy, his Boy Scout experience might have provided a subculture that significantly affected his life. This category also includes particular church or parachurch cultures. For people who strongly identify with a particular subculture, its effect on their heritage may be great.

A person's heritage is both concrete and developing. Looking back at our past, we can see an unchangeable history of experiences in various environments. At the same time, our current experiences and environment are shaping our heritage of tomorrow.

Heritage affects the way people relate with others and fulfill their roles. For instance, people who have been in environments where emotions are expressed through physical contact will likely respond differently than those whose backgrounds are primarily verbal. It's helpful, then, to understand other people's heritages as well as our own. In order to grow in our ability to love others, we must understand the "heritage lens" through which *we* view life as well as the "lenses" through which *others* see life.

Conclusion

This session neither exalts nor condemns someone's heritage. The primary objectives are to acknowledge our heritage and learn how it affects our identity. God has sovereignly placed us where He desires us to be. It is only appropriate that we thank Him for our lives and what He plans to do in, through, and with them.

Assignment

Read *Session 6: Values*.

Complete the *Life Inventory: Values II* exercise beginning on page 114.

Time Alone with God

Our next session will tackle values and get to the core of why we do what we do. Therefore, now would be a great time for you to be alone with God and reflect on your values. A time of solitude is ideal for doing the "Life Inventory: Values II" exercise, which asks you to be honest with yourself about your real values in your daily living. Here is a suggested plan for using this time alone with God.

Pray

Spend time in silence, prayer, and worship. Focus on God and enjoy His presence. Consider the profound reality that God, who is above and beyond all earthly things, has touched our lives as believers through the work of Christ. Enter into God's presence, reflect on His glory, and communicate your praise to Him. You may choose to spend some time reading and thinking over some passages from Scripture, or you may just spend some quiet time in worship or prayer.

Reflect on "Values II"

In your "Values I" exercise, you've already written your twelve most deeply held values. Use the "Values II" exercise beginning on page 121 to validate your values with specific actions from your life. Think through your life (weekly schedule, relationships, work, ministry, studies) and consider how your life "proves" each value you hold. Write down actions you consistently do that reflect each of your twelve values from the "Values I" section.

Do this with complete honesty before God. You may not be able to substantiate some values. Those are values that you wish were priorities but that you don't practice as much as you'd like.

Next, go back through your list of values and mark each value as real (values consistent with the way you live) or ideal (values you hold in an idealistic way but can't validate from patterns in your behavior).

Finally, meditate on what you've discovered and ask God these questions:

- Are the values I listed godly values?
- How do You want me to change my ideal values into real values? How can I trust You to help me?
- What other values do You want me to have?

Review

Close with some time in prayer and journal writing. Reflect on what you've learned about your identity, and write down any insight from God that your time alone has revealed.

Values

Enquiring within, and boldly searching into one's own Bosom, must
be the most shocking Employment, that a Man can give his Mind
to, whose greatest Pleasure consists in secretly admiring himself.
—Bernard Mandeville, "Second Dialogue," *The Fable of the Bees*

Having examined various aspects of our earthly identity (roles, gender,
temperament, and heritage), now we will look at our values. Our values
are near the core of our identity. They are the things we judge to be good
for us and others.

Our earthly identity has shaped much of what we value. Later in this study
we'll ask, "Because my earthly identity has embedded many of my values
deep within me, how do I discern which values need to change now that
I'm a follower of Christ?" We'll address this question when we investigate
our heavenly identity. The Spirit of God, who resides in your life, will illu-
minate for you how your values need to change. For now, we will simply
ask what personal values are and what part they play in our identity.

Session Aims

Individual Aim: To gain a greater understanding of your own values, the
implications of such values, and the necessity of prioritizing them wisely
before God.

Group Aim: To begin fostering trust through honest sharing of personal
values and their implications in group members' lives.

Preparation

Read *Session 6: Values*.

Complete the *Life Inventory: Values II* exercise beginning on page 114.

Introduction

In Psalm 19, David declares the greatness of God's law. As he describes the law's nature, benefits, and effects, he makes a value statement about these ordinances. David says,

> The fear of the LORD is pure,
>   enduring forever.
> The ordinances of the LORD are sure
>   and altogether righteous.
> They are more precious than gold,
>   than much pure gold;
> they are sweeter than honey,
>   than honey from the comb. (verses 9-10)

This statement expresses David's values, as well as those of his culture. Gold and honey were of great value. To own gold, build with gold, or craft things in gold was valued. The sweetness of honey was also highly valued. But although David valued these things as anyone else would, he valued something else far more: the law of the Lord. Because this value was greater, he would prefer the law and its benefits to the benefits of gold and honey.

In the same way, we must prioritize our values because the way that we rank our values will determine how we live.

Content

The apostle Paul says we are both God's building and God's builder. First, the whole community of God's people is the temple or holy house where God dwells (see Ephesians 2:19-22). And each individual believer is God's temple too: "Don't you know that you yourselves are God's temple and that God's Spirit lives in you?" (1 Corinthians 3:16).

At the same time, each of us is also a builder of God's temple: "If any man builds on this foundation [that is, Christ as proclaimed in the apostle's teaching] using gold, silver, costly stones, wood, hay or straw, his work will be shown for what it is, because the Day will bring it to light" (1 Corinthians 3:12-13). We each must choose how we will build our own lives. Each day we can build upon the foundation of Christ that has already been laid. As we build, we choose what materials to build with.

Verses 12-13 imply that we should value certain materials over others. Depending upon what we value, we will find reward or loss (see verses 14-15). For example, if a man values social status, he will build his life in a certain way. He will pursue a certain level of income to afford a certain type of car and a home in a certain kind of neighborhood. If he is in jeopardy of not attaining those things or of losing them once attained, his value of them may cause him to practice questionable business ethics in order to protect his status and possessions. He may do whatever it takes to obtain and retain his status. Secret, unethical behavior that bolsters his status seems okay. Someone who lives like this has built his life, so to speak, with stubble. In the end, it counts for nothing before God and in the scheme of eternity.

The previous work we did on gender, temperament, and heritage sheds light on our values. For instance, the man who values social status may have carried this value with him from his family culture. It may have been his parents' normal mode of operation. In fact, he may not even know how influential this value is to him until someone points it out or until he spends time reflecting on his life. Or maybe status is part of his understanding of manhood. Perhaps his dad modeled to him that being a man entails building and protecting a certain respectability in the community. (Maybe his sister doesn't hold this value because their family didn't value status for a daughter.)

Finally, this value could stem from his temperament. He may have an inborn inclination to be driven toward success. If the only way success has been defined in his life is in terms of social status, he will tend to pursue that with all the diligence he can muster.

You may know someone who resembles this man, or you may be like him yourself. But we've portrayed him in a one-dimensional perspective. A second look at this example surfaces a crucial characteristic of personal values. In the example, we assumed that this man would place a greater priority of value on his social status than on his integrity in business. In reality, many competing values often influence our decisions. It's not evil to have some degree of concern with how you fit in socially. For instance, dressing according to last decade's fashions may place unnecessary barriers between you and others (even though dressing according to *two* decades previous may make you fashionable!). So our real challenge is to decide what we hold at various degrees of importance according to the standard of Christ.

A simple but helpful definition of a value is: "something (as a principle or quality) intrinsically valuable or desirable."[1] At one level, values are the ideals, customs, and institutions of a society. When judged by a biblical standard, these values may be positive (education, freedom), neutral (cleanliness), or negative (cruelty, crime, blasphemy). We can also think of values as objects or qualities that are desirable as ends in themselves. Every person holds a unique set of values.

People often express their values in a word or phrase. (All politicians say they value "the family.") But if we want to adequately evaluate our lives, it's better to express values in a phrase or sentence. (A politician would be clearer by saying, "A family led by two moms or two dads is no family at all.")

When someone uses a single word to tell us what they value, we can interpret it in a variety of ways. That's why it's often hard to understand what people mean when they say they value something. The goal in this session is to understand your own and others' values accurately. For instance, the man discussed previously may say he values "respectability." However, if we spell out his value in a sentence, based on his behavior, it might be, "I will do whatever it takes at work to obtain and retain social respectability in my community."

So do your best to consider not just what you value but exactly how you express those values in your life. Clarifying your values in your own mind will help you put into words how and why a particular value is expressed in your life.

Conclusion

What we value is of utmost significance to how we live. We need to be honest with ourselves about our real values. Identifying them helps us evaluate whether we're living out our values in godly ways. For example, someone may say he values punctuality. But if what he means is that if anyone is late to meet him, he won't meet with that person again, he may not be expressing a value of punctuality in a godly way. Our heavenly identity needs to influence our values. We need to see how our earthly identity may be influencing our values in ways that are inconsistent with our identity in Christ.

The good man brings good things out of the good stored up in his heart, and the evil man brings evil things out of the evil stored up in his heart. For out of the overflow of his heart his mouth speaks. (Luke 6:45)

Remember that our hearts will follow what we value!

Assignment

Read *Session 7: Identity in Christ.*

Complete the *Life Inventory: Identity in Christ* exercise beginning on page 116.

Complete *Biblical Exercise: Ephesians 1–2* beginning on page 61.

Identity in Christ

In session 6, we talked about values. Much of what we value stems from the various aspects of identity discussed thus far. Our gender, temperament, and heritage all affect our understanding of our world and ourselves and, therefore, affect our values. However, as we enter into a relationship with Christ, we are challenged to reevaluate our values and how we prioritize them.

Session Aims

Individual Aim: To begin an exploration of the magnificent depths of your identity in Christ.

Group Aim: To discuss the implications of identity in Christ on group members' lives.

Preparation

Read *Session 7: Identity in Christ.*

Complete the *Life Inventory: Identity in Christ* exercise beginning on page 116.

Complete *Biblical Exercise: Ephesians 1–2* beginning on page 61.

Introduction

We are dual citizens: of earth and of heaven. As we realize this, we feel our heavenly identity crashing down on our earthly identity. We will spend a lifetime scrutinizing how we prioritize our values in light of our commitment to follow Christ. As we do so, our heavenly values will sometimes affirm, sometimes modify, and sometimes completely reject our earthly values.

Let's look at this heavenly identity, which is best known as our identity in Christ.

Content

In his letters, the apostle Paul often used the expression "in Christ." Although we can't come close to addressing the breadth of this phrase in our session, we want to look at a fundamental aspect of being "in Christ." To be "in Christ" means to share in Christ's death and resurrection, and to be placed under the headship of Christ rather than Adam means that we now live with a completely different attitude toward everything we do. These ideas are laid out in Romans 5:12-21 and 6:1-11.

As you read through the list of characteristics in the "Life Inventory: Identity in Christ" exercise, you might not be "moved" by the significance of each one. There are several reasons why not: (1) Lists can be dull and impersonal, (2) each truth carries more weight than a simple declaration can capture, (3) you might not understand some statements, or (4) even though you understand and affirm each truth, they may seem distant and even irrelevant to your life right now. The last two reasons are worth looking into further.

Understanding our identity in Christ is critical to a fruitful walk with the Lord. The central events of Christianity, Christ's death and resurrection, are the foundation of the Christian life. Dying with Christ means dying to the things that used to run our lives. For instance, while material wealth is the central motivation in many people's lives, Christ calls us to relinquish pursuing wealth as a core motivation. The same is true of any other vice that keeps us from fully loving God and people.

Rising with Christ means rising to a new way of living under His kingship. Before we came under Christ's kingship, our identity was dominated by concerns other than loving God and loving people as Jesus did. There was no way we could transform ourselves to make us acceptable to our perfect Judge and Maker. Whether we knew it or not, objectives and motivations that didn't focus on loving God and others were running our lives.

Certainly, our earthly identity may contain characteristics that influenced us in godly ways. For instance, our parents may have taught us to be honest. Yet sin and offensive independence from God characterized our lives. Ironically, this "independence" was evidence of Adam's control. When we come under Christ's kingship, by God's grace through our faith, we gain a heavenly component to our identity.

To say that we have a new component is a gross understatement. Coming under Christ's kingship ought to so transform our understanding of our identity that, in many respects, we no longer consider ourselves the same people. We are new creatures (see 2 Corinthians 5:17). (For more on how we pursue transformation according to our heavenly identity, see the study called *Integrity* in this series.) The most basic truth of our identity, our position before God, is determined by who our King is, even though Adam's realm may still influence us. And our actions will reflect our participation in one kingdom or the other, for each kingdom has certain "deeds" or "fruit" characteristic of it. The deeds of the flesh (see Galatians 5:19-21) result from being in Adam, whereas the fruit of the Spirit (see Galatians 5:22-23) grows when we are in Christ.

What does it mean to be under Christ's kingship? To be under a king is to be subject to that king's will. In our fallen world, that concept rarely sounds appealing. After all, who would agree to be entirely subject to someone else's will? Would you approach a stranger and say, "I'm at your disposal, and I'll do anything you want me to do"? Our minds immediately race through all the abuses that might result from such a scenario. That's because we don't trust strangers. As subjects of Christ's kingdom, though, we face an entirely different scenario. We have come to know Him and have found that His will is love. As subjects of Christ, we are implored to do His will, which involves actively caring for others, as pointed out in 1 John:

> *Dear friends, let us love one another, for love comes from God. Everyone who loves has been born of God and knows God. Whoever does not love does not know God, because God is love. This is how God showed his love among us: He sent his one and only Son into the world that we might live through him. This is love: not that we loved God, but that he loved us and sent his Son as an atoning sacrifice for our sins. Dear friends, since God so loved us, we also ought to love one another. No one has ever seen God; but if we love one another, God lives in us and his love is made complete in us. (4:7-12)*

> *If anyone has material possessions and sees his brother in need but has no pity on him, how can the love of God be in him? Dear children, let us not love with words or tongue but with actions and in truth. (3:17-18)*

Many people think being saved is like eternal life insurance. It's more like a pledge of allegiance to a new King. Our Sovereign God doesn't compel us to produce something for Him that He lacks. Our allegiance to Him requires us simply to love our fellow subjects actively and also to love those who claim no such allegiance—our King's enemies. How strange this kingdom is to a world that understands the love of friends but knows nothing of loving enemies! But the world has not experienced the love of Christ. We love those who are not followers of our King because we realize that they may simply be enemies who have not yet become brothers. We love fellow believers because we share the joy of being loved by our Great King and we are, therefore, now brothers. We believers are individuals in a community marked by Love, whose name is Jesus.

Conclusion

We have only scratched the surface of our identity in Christ. Though it will take a lifetime to plunge its depths, it's worth your time and energy to make such an exploration. For instance, what does it mean for you, personally, to live a life characterized mainly by love? You will examine part of the answer to that question in session 9, where you'll consider your spiritual gifts. Through exercising your giftedness as a member of the body of Christ, you'll learn how your way of loving others has a unique focus.

The features of your earthly identity will also affect the way you love others. However, the first thing you'll find if you seek to live up to the standard of love is that you won't attain to that standard as Christ did. As a result, you may begin to ask yourself, *Am I still a sinner who will be free from sinning only after death?*

Biblical Exercise: Ephesians 1–2

Read Ephesians 1:1–2:22. Also, review "A Method for the Biblical Exercises" beginning on page 17.

Observation — **"What Do I See?"**

1. Who are the persons (including God) in the passage? What is the condition of those persons?

2. What subjects did Paul discuss in the passage? What did he assert?

3. Note the sequence in which Paul made these assertions. (You might number them in order.)

4. What did Paul emphasize? Are there repeated ideas and themes? How are the various parts related?

5. Why did Paul write this passage? (Did he say anything about ways he expected the reader to change after reading it?)

Interpretation Phase 1 — "What Did It Mean Then?"

1. Coming to Terms—Are there any words in the passage that you don't understand? Write down anything you found confusing about the passage.

2. Finding Where It Fits—What clues does the Bible give about the meaning of this passage?

- Immediate Context (the passage being studied)

- Remote Context (passages that come before and after the one being studied)

3. Getting into Their Sandals—An Exercise in Imagination

- What are the main points of this passage? Summarize or write an outline of it.

- What do you think the recipients of the letter were supposed to take from this passage? How did God, inspiring Paul to write Ephesians, want this passage to impact the Ephesian believers?

Interpretation Phase 2 — **"What Does It Mean Now?"**

1. What is the timeless truth in the passage? In one or two sentences, write down what you learned about God from Ephesians 1–2.

2. How does that truth work today?

Application — "What Can I Do to Make This Truth Real?"

1. What can I do to make this truth real for myself?

2. For my family?

3. For my friends?

4. For the people who live near me?

5. For the rest of the world?

Assignment

Read *Session 8: Saint or Sinner.*

Complete *Biblical Exercise: 1 Peter 1–2* beginning on page 70.

Saint or Sinner

As we continue to look at our identity in Christ, we must settle on how we will fundamentally view ourselves during our stay on earth. Our central characteristic, love for God and others, is a standard that is virtually impossible to attain. Thus, we often find ourselves falling short of loving God and others. Are we sinners who are forgiven, or saints who still sin? When we go to the very foundation of our identity as Christians who still reside in a fallen world, do we find depravity or righteousness?

Session Aims

Individual Aim: To consider your status and nature based on the Scripture's definitions of saint and sinner.

Group Aim: To review and evaluate the nature of a Christian as it relates to sin and righteousness.

Preparation

Read *Session 8: Saint or Sinner*.

Complete *Biblical Exercise: 1 Peter 1–2* beginning on page 70.

Introduction

On the surface, asking whether we are saved sinners or sinning saints may appear to be splitting hairs, but the ramifications of the answers are vast. Too often we judge our status based on recent behavior. If we go through a time of significant sinfulness, we view ourselves as hopelessly trapped by the dominion of sin. Likewise, if we experience a time of spiritual growth and restraint from sinful behavior, we are more prone to see ourselves as worthy of the designation "saint." We need to build our identity upon the definition of Scripture rather than upon our feelings about, or analysis of, our lifestyle.

Content

Sinner or saint? While a fair examination of Scripture finds both descriptions, the point of this session is to find out why and in what sense we are both saints and sinners.

The New Testament describes Christians as growing in holiness while also struggling with sin. Yet our struggle with sin doesn't undermine our firm standing before God when we have trusted Christ for salvation (see Romans 5:9-11). Because of our new identity in Christ, we're called to be holy because God is holy (see 1 Peter 1:16). *Holy* means "separated out for a special purpose." We are separated out from others simply in that others haven't been reconciled to God through Christ. *Saint* means "holy person" or "one who is separated out." So we're saints in that we've been separated out for special purposes: worshiping God, abandoning sin, and living in ways that draw others toward Christ.

Christ is the ultimate Saint because the rest of us fall short of the perfection He attained as God in human flesh. Yet Christians are identified with Christ by grace through faith in Him. Our identity is radically changed.

But how are believers changed? The short answer is: over time and through experiences. One major change is that we learn a new way to decide what is good. We've acknowledged that God's righteousness (His standard of what is true, just, and good) is now the goal of our life. After all, a true commitment to Christ involves repenting of our failure to live up to God's righteousness and receiving the gift of righteousness in Christ.

Look at the difference between the rich young ruler (see Mark 10:17-23) and Zacchaeus (see Luke 19:1-10). The ruler was unwilling to repent from valuing money and its benefits above God's righteousness. His life didn't change because his fundamental values remained unchanged. Zacchaeus, on the other hand, decided to repent of his primary pursuit of money and, in exchange, acknowledge his need to live according to God's righteous standards. He received grace and forgiveness from Jesus but also a fundamental shift in how he perceived his life purpose. Internally, his values had already shifted to the point that he began pouring out his estate to those he had wronged.

We shouldn't presume that Zacchaeus went on to live a sinless life. However, we can see that his fundamental understanding of life had radically changed. He had a new understanding of himself and his purpose because Christ had offered him new life.

This is why James emphasized the manifestation of faith in a person's behavior ("faith without deeds is dead"; see James 2:14-26). James meant that a Christian's life can't possibly be void of righteous behavior. Growth in righteousness may at times seem stagnant, but there's always some evidence of transformation in a believer's values and behavior over a significant period of time. If our life is void of righteousness, we can't have repented of our past life in favor of valuing God's righteous standard. In other words, we wouldn't really be believers. We are fundamentally changed only when we genuinely come to faith in Christ. And if we have genuinely come to faith, our prospect for life after death will always be changed *and*, here in this life, our life in Christ will always be changing.

Conclusion

Calling ourselves saints doesn't ignore the sin in every believer's life. Believers still sin. This diminishes neither the holy standard God has set nor the sinfulness of believers who fail to meet that standard. Although believers sin, faith in Christ changes a person so radically in God's eyes that the title of saint is appropriate.

One part of having their identity fundamentally changed is that believers receive "gifts" with which to serve others. God gifts each believer uniquely for His service. We will discuss spiritual gifts in the next session.

Biblical Exercise: 1 Peter 1–2

Read 1 Peter 1:3–2:3. Also, review "A Method for the Biblical Exercises" beginning on page 17.

Observation — "What Do I See?"

1. Who are the persons (including God) in the passage? What is the condition of those persons?

2. What subjects did Peter discuss in the passage? What did he assert?

3. Note the sequence in which Peter made these assertions. (You might number them in order.)

4. What did Peter emphasize? Are there repeated ideas and themes? How are the various parts related?

5. Why did Peter write this passage? (Did he say anything about ways he expected the reader to change after reading it?)

Interpretation Phase 1 — "What Did It Mean Then?"

1. Coming to Terms — Are there any words in the passage that you don't understand? Write down anything you found confusing about the passage.

2. Finding Where It Fits—What clues does the Bible give about the meaning of this passage?

   - Immediate Context (the passage being studied)

   - Remote Context (passages that come before and after the one being studied)

3. Getting into Their Sandals—An Exercise in Imagination

   - What are the main points of this passage? Summarize or write an outline of the passage.

   - What do you think the recipients of the letter were supposed to take from this passage? How did God, inspiring Peter to write this letter, want this passage to impact the recipients?

Interpretation Phase 2 — **"What Does It Mean Now?"**

1. What is the timeless truth in the passage? In one or two sentences, write down what you learned about God from 1 Peter 1–2.

2. How does that truth work today?

Application — **"What Can I Do to Make This Truth Real?"**

1. What can I do to make this truth real for myself?

2. For my family?

3. For my friends?

4. For the people who live near me?

5. For the rest of the world?

Assignment

Read *Session 9: Spiritual Gifts*.

Complete the *Life Inventory: Spiritual Gifts* exercise beginning on page 118.

Spiritual Gifts

We have discovered aspects of identity in Christ that are shared by all believers. Christ's kingdom is a commonality that unites us together powerfully. But this unity doesn't mean uniformity. Part of being in Christ means having a unique identity and function within the Christian community. We will now explore some of these distinguishing characteristics as we take a look at our spiritual gifts.

Session Aims

Individual Aim: To gain greater clarity about your spiritual gifts and how you can use those gifts in service to the community for the glory of Christ.

Group Aim: To see how the giftedness of different members contributes to their individual identity and to the community's presentation of Christ to the world.

Preparation

Read *Session 9: Spiritual Gifts*.

Complete the *Life Inventory: Spiritual Gifts* exercise beginning on page 118.

Introduction

One key to determining your spiritual gifts is recognizing the times when you've effectively served others and received affirmation. You may have a breadth of ministry experience from church or parachurch ministries, or you may have little or no ministry experience. Whether this is your first attempt to identify your spiritual gifts or one of many attempts, the process of identifying your gifts can help you better serve in the body of Christ. If "ministry" seems too grand a word, try seeing your gifts as means of expressing Christ's love to others. As more and more believers exercise their gifts, the community increasingly becomes a representation of Christ to the watching world. Outsiders come to faith when they see such a community of faith.

Content

There are many helpful aids in understanding our giftedness. But before we seek to identify what gifts we may or may not have, we need to commit to honesty with ourselves and humbly put our lives in proper perspective before God. As Romans 12:3 instructs, we are to view ourselves with sober judgment according to the measure of faith given to us. Gifts differ according to the grace given to us (see Romans 12:6). God freely gives us our gifts at our spiritual rebirth in the same way He gave our natural talents at our physical birth. Because we don't earn or create our own gifts, there's no room for pride, comparison, or envy about gifts we may or may not have. "Spiritual gifts are given in Christ; they are enrichments received from Christ. It is vital that we should see this, or we shall be confusing natural and spiritual gifts to the end of our days."[1]

Christ ought to be central in our thinking about the Spirit's ministry through us:

> The truth we must grasp here is that our exercise of spiritual gifts is nothing more nor less than Christ himself ministering through his body to his body, to the Father, and to all mankind. From heaven Christ uses Christians as his mouth, his hands, his feet, even his smile; it is through us, his people, that he speaks and acts, meets, loves, and saves here and now in this world. This seems (though the point is disputed) to be part of the meaning of Paul's picture of the church as Christ's body, in which every believer is a "member" in the sense of a limb or organ: The head is the command center for the body, and the limbs move at the head's direction.[2]

You may be starting from scratch in trying to discern what gifts you have to offer others. If so, don't feel ashamed. Instead, look around you; consider what ministries are happening in your local church body and perhaps what ministries are not. Begin by picking a ministry that you are drawn to, and inquire about how you can serve. As you jump in and begin serving others, it will become apparent over time in what areas you are and are not gifted.

Conclusion

Just as we discovered universal and unique aspects of our earthly identity (gender, temperament, and heritage), we also find corporate and individual distinctions in our heavenly identity in Christ. While discovering individual distinctions is helpful, our discussion of giftedness is not an end in itself. The end is the shared maturity of the entire community of believers. Our identity in Christ intimately bonds us to other believers in the pursuit of becoming like Christ (see Ephesians 4:11-16).

Assignment

Read *Session 10: Corporate Aspects of Identity in Christ.*

Complete *Biblical Exercise: Colossians 3* beginning on page 83.

Corporate Aspects of Identity in Christ

As we probe the depths of our identity in Christ, we want to direct our attention to a phrase in one of Paul's letters: "the new man." Our look into the meaning of "the old man" and "the new man" (see Colossians 3:9-10) will reveal that our identity is not only individual but also corporate. This is a significant biblical discovery as we close our study of *Identity*.

Session Aims

Individual Aim: To gain a greater understanding of and appreciation for Christian community.

Group Aim: To explore the corporate aspects of identity in Christ and discuss the implications of each aspect of our new identity.

Preparation

Read *Session 10: Corporate Aspects of Identity in Christ*.

Complete *Biblical Exercise: Colossians 3* beginning on page 83.

Introduction

As we noted in the session about heritage, our culture greatly affects the way we view our identity and the world around us. Our culture can even influence our initial interpretation of Scripture. Often those who have been raised in an individualistic culture view the phrase "in Christ" primarily as an individual experience rather than a corporate one. But that's not how Paul intended it.

Content

Christian identity is inherently corporate. More often than not, the New Testament writers speak of identity in Christ in plural terms. Almost all of the pronouns in the great identity chapters of Ephesians are in the plural. Even the second person "you" in those sections is plural in the original Greek, which, unlike English, has a different word for "you" singular than "you" plural. Those who grow up in a Western culture are often blind to the corporate way the Bible presents the believer's identity in Christ:

> American culture is obsessed with the individual. Individual rights are the cornerstone of many cultural truths we hold dear. The image of the strong individual moving west of the thirteen original colonies to claim both land and a future is a powerful theme in the early American history. "Rugged American individualism" is a phrase we learn at a young age.[1]

One biblical metaphor for Christian identity that is usually interpreted individually is the "new man" and the "old man." The New International Version translates Colossians 3:9-10 like this:

> *Do not lie to each other, since you have taken off your old self with its practices and have put on the new self, which is being renewed in knowledge in the image of its Creator.*

"Old self" and "new self" here are literally "old man" and "new man." The New English Translation renders the passage like this:

> *Do not lie to one another since you have put off the old man with its practices and have been clothed with the new man that is being renewed in knowledge according to the image of the one who created it.*

"Self" in the New International Version is a clearly individualistic reading of this passage. It's defensible, especially if one has been steeped in the psychological revolution of the twentieth century. However, there's reason to believe that we've misunderstood that phrase. New Testament scholar Darrell Bock points out that Colossians 3 uses second person plurals ("you" as a group rather than "you" as an individual). Bock thinks the "new man" may refer not to individual believers but to the whole body of a church community. Here he summarizes his analysis:

> So the new man is related to Christ and consists of peoples. In other words, it is Christ conceived of as a corporate entity, that is, Christ's body. Another way to say it is that the new man refers to the new community in Christ that he forms by joining people to himself as they are saved (i.e., "buried and raised with him," as Paul already declared in Colossians). An even simpler way to say it is that the new man is the church, the new community in Christ.[2]

If Bock is right, then a core part of a Christian's identity is his or her connection to a community of other believers. In the same way that our earthly identity involves a nonnegotiable connection to other persons, whom we call our family, our heavenly identity binds us to a heavenly family. We cannot deny that we are and will remain "family" with our biological parents and siblings. While in recent years biological family bonds have been weakened and broken (at least in legal terms), one's earthly father, mother, and siblings will always be so. Likewise, though believers may avoid contact with a local church community, at the core of their identity they are to be members of a larger community of Christians. When believers fail to be or are restricted from being involved with that corporate experience, then a part of their identity is distorted.

Consider the prayer of Christ on the night of His betrayal:

> "My prayer is not for them [his first disciples] alone. I pray also for those who will believe in me through their message, that all of them may be one, Father, just as you are in me and I am in you. May they also be in us so that the world may believe that you have sent me. I have given them the glory that you gave me, that they may be one as we are one: I in them and you in me. May they be brought to complete unity to let the world know that you sent me and have loved them even as you have loved me.

> "Father, I want those you have given me to be with me where I am, and to see my glory, the glory you have given me because you loved me before the creation of the world.

"Righteous Father, though the world does not know you, I know you, and they know that you have sent me. I have made you known to them, and will continue to make you known in order that the love you have for me may be in them and that I myself may be in them." (John 17:20-26, emphasis added)

The analogy here is powerful. Just as Jesus' identity is inextricably linked with His Father's identity, so a Christian's identity is to be linked with a community of other believers. Jesus' prayer is that we be completely one, just as He and God the Father are one. Clearly, intimate involvement in community with other believers is nonnegotiable for Christians.

Conclusion

Having considered a few biblical references to corporate Christian identity, we see that a concept of identity that is limited to an isolated individual is incomplete. As members of the body of Christ, we have the privilege of sharing a heavenly identity that will bind us together for eternity. Our earthly relationships, then, serve as a significant context for our growth and God's glory.

Biblical Exercise: Colossians 3

Read Colossians 3:1-25. Also, review "A Method for the Biblical Exercises" beginning on page 17.

Observation — **"What Do I See?"**

1. Who are the persons (including God) in the passage? What is the condition of those persons?

2. What subjects did Paul discuss in the passage? What did he assert?

3. Note the sequence in which Paul made these assertions. (You might number them in order.)

4. What did Paul emphasize? Are there repeated ideas and themes? How are the various parts related?

5. Why did Paul write this passage? (Did he say anything about ways he expected the reader to change after reading it?)

Interpretation Phase 1 — **"What Did It Mean Then?"**

1. Coming to Terms—Are there any words in the passage that you don't understand? Write down anything you found confusing about the passage.

2. Finding Where It Fits—What clues does the Bible give about the meaning of this passage?

   - Immediate Context (the passage being studied)

   - Remote Context (passages that come before and after the one being studied)

3. Getting into Their Sandals—An Exercise in Imagination

   - What are the main points of this passage? Summarize or write an outline of the passage.

- What do you think the recipients of the letter were supposed to take from this passage? How did God, inspiring Paul to write this letter, want this passage to impact the recipients?

Interpretation Phase 2 — **"What Does It Mean Now?"**

1. What is the timeless truth in the passage? In one or two sentences, write down what you learned about God from Colossians 3.

2. How does that truth work today?

Application — **"What Can I Do to Make This Truth Real?"**

1. What can I do to make this truth real for myself?

2. For my family?

3. For my friends?

4. For the people who live near me?

5. For the rest of the world?

Life Inventory

Introduction

"Life Inventory" will help you identify your personal characteristics in various categories. Thinking about the aspects of your life and then writing them on paper takes time and energy, but you'll get out of the experience as much as you put into it.

You'll analyze your earthly identity first. Your earthly identity involves things that both unbelievers and believers share, such as roles, gender, temperament, and heritage. Next you'll look at your personal values as you transition into thinking about your heavenly identity. Your heavenly identity is who you are as a result of having trusted in Christ.

You'll do the "Life Inventory" exercises on your own, outside your group meetings. Then you'll share with your group the highlights of what you've learned. You don't have to share anything you don't want to. However, you'll find that sharing your findings with your group will strengthen your friendships with each other.

Roles

Roles and Responsibilities

Review the sample chart that follows. Then, in the empty chart, record the roles you currently hold. These may include your role as an employee, husband or wife, father or mother, church member, citizen, participant in a sport, and so on. Adjacent to your list of roles, describe the responsibilities that you hold in that role. For example, as a citizen of the United States, you are responsible to obey the laws, participate in voting for representatives in government, and serve on a jury when called. This exercise is simply an inventory of your life regarding your roles and their corresponding responsibilities.

Roles	Responsibilities
Husband	Remain faithful to my wife, provide protection for her, provide companionship for her
Father	Protect and provide financially for my kids, train them to be responsible and loving
School Teacher	Clearly teach my subject, maintain an orderly classroom, motivate students by personal interaction and respect, give assignments, prepare exercises, grade homework, fill out paperwork, meet with parents
Little League Coach	Prepare drills for practice, attend practices, maintain equipment, motivate team members to do their best, teach teamwork and skills, coach games
U.S. Citizen	Prepare tax forms, pay taxes, be an informed voter, know and obey laws, stay informed of current events, go to jury duty when called

Roles	Responsibilities

Spiritual Discipline Exercise — Simplicity

Simplicity has been widely recognized in the Christian tradition as a discipline. The "Roles" exercise provides an ideal opportunity to ask yourself, *Is my life adequately simplified?* Take some time to pray and reflect on the roles and responsibilities you currently hold. Seek wisdom from your time of prayer and from trusted believers. Do you have roles that you are convinced God is guiding you to perform but that require you to simplify other areas of life in order for you to fulfill these roles well? Are there roles that you hold but do not feel guided by God to perform? Are there too many distractions in your life that hinder you from giving your full attention to your roles? Make a list below of steps you will take to simplify your life.

Gender

This exercise will help you discover where some of your perspectives about gender have come from in the context of your earthly identity. In other words, how and from whom did you learn what masculinity and femininity are?

Respond to the following questions as objectively as you can. Both men and women should answer every question.

1. Would you describe your dad as having been primarily present or absent during your childhood? Explain.

2. What did your dad's life teach you about what it means to be a man?

3. How did your dad relate to your mom?

4. Was there ever a time when your dad acknowledged that you had become a man or a woman? If yes, how did he do so? What criteria did he use (to your knowledge)?

5. Would you describe your mom as empowering or controlling? Explain.

6. How much time did you spend with your mom?

7. What did your mom's life teach you about what it means to be a woman?

8. How did your mom relate to your dad?

9. Was there ever a time when your mom acknowledged that you had become a man or a woman? If yes, how did she do so? What criteria did she use (to your knowledge)?

10. From infancy through your teen years, were most of the adults you spent significant time with men or women? (Think of relatives, parents' friends, teachers, and coaches.)

11. How did these adults' views on masculinity and femininity compare with your parents' views?

12. When you were a child, were your friends mainly male or female? What about when you were a teen?

13. During your childhood, how did you distinguish between boys and girls?

14. What did your peers understand about masculinity and femininity?

15. What are the main things you learned about gender during your childhood and early adult life?

Temperament

Although there are many personality assessment approaches, we will use the Myers-Briggs Type Indicator. David Keirsey and Marilyn Bates, in their book *Please Understand Me*, provide summary charts of MBTI's four categories of human personality. The charts on the following pages are based on charts and descriptions from *Please Understand Me*.[1] Carefully read through the charts and consider which characteristics are generally accurate for you.

Paul Tieger and Barbara Barron-Tieger, in their book *Do What You Are*, warn not to "worry too much about the terms used to describe the four dimensions (for example, 'Sensing' versus 'Intuition'). In some sense, these terms don't mean exactly what you think they do. Although they are words you know, they mean something different in this context."[2] The goal of this exercise is to begin to notice some basic characteristics of your personality that are consistent patterns in your behavior. The process will help you see that other people have different tendencies to how they respond to certain circumstances, just as much as you do. An awareness of that can be extremely helpful in our endeavor as followers of Christ to love others well.

Check or circle the descriptions that you think fit your personality, and make any applicable notes in the margins for your own reference. Then, write down answers to the questions that follow each chart. Keirsey and Bates encourage us to remember that you are looking for the predominant response in your life—the tendency. "The question always arises, 'Does not an extravert also have an introverted side and does not an introvert also have an extraverted side?' Yes, of course. But the preferred attitude, whether it be extraversion or introversion, will have the most potency and the other will be the 'suppressed minority.'"[3]

We need to stress that this exercise and its use of these charts will not by itself verify your personality type. This exercise merely gives you a chance to consider what your type may be and to think about how knowing your type can help you live out your faith. (For a complete understanding of personality type and an effective method for verifying your personality type, see *Please Understand Me*.)

Extraverts/Introverts

1. Circle the traits that best describe you:

Extraverts	**Introverts**
Energized by social settings	Drained by social settings
Concern for external world and others	Concern for internal condition or reaction
Quantity of relationships	Quality of relationships
Prefer breadth	Prefer depth
Lonely when isolated from people	Lonely when surrounded by strangers
Drained by private time and space	Energized by private time and space
Prefer group interaction	Prefer focused concentration
Many friends	Limited friends

2. How do the characteristics you circled challenge your ability to be loving toward others?

3. How do they contribute positively toward your ability to be loving toward others?

4. How do they affect (both positively and negatively) your endeavor to live in a godly manner?

5. How do they affect your relationship with God?

Sensors/Intuitives

6. Circle the traits that best describe you:

Sensors	Intuitives
Rely on experience	Rely on hunches
Realistic	Speculative
Actual	Possible
What is	What if?
Down-to-earth	Head-in-clouds
Sensible	Imaginative
Trust facts	Suspicious of facts
Gathers facts	Considers options
Remembers facts	Seeks to overcome facts
Concern with past	Concern with future
Patterns	Change

7. How do the characteristics you circled challenge your ability to be loving toward others?

8. How do they contribute positively toward your ability to be loving toward others?

9. How do they affect (both positively and negatively) your endeavor to live in a godly manner?

10. How do they affect your relationship with God?

Thinkers/Feelers

11. Circle the traits that best describe you:

Thinkers	Feelers
Objective	Subjective
Principles	Values
Policy	Social values
Laws	Extenuating circumstances
Impersonal	Personal
Analysis	Sympathy
Justice	Humane
Hard-headed	Soft-hearted
Embarrassed to show emotion	Show emotion naturally
Persuaded by "rightness"	Persuaded by effect on others

12. How do the characteristics you circled challenge your ability to be loving toward others?

13. How do they contribute positively toward your ability to be loving toward others?

14. How do they affect (both positively and negatively) your endeavor to live in a godly manner?

15. How do they affect your relationship with God?

Judgers/Perceivers

16. Circle the traits that best describe you:

Judgers	**Perceivers**
Decided	Gather more data
Fixed	Flexible
Plan ahead	Adapt as they go
Run one's life	Let life happen
Decision making	Treasure hunting
Planned	Open-ended
Wrap it up	Something will turn up
Deadline!	What deadline?
Make lists	Just wing it
Get the show on the road	Let's wait and see

17. How do the characteristics you circled challenge your ability to be loving toward others?

18. How do they contribute positively toward your ability to be loving toward others?

19. How do they affect (both positively and negatively) your endeavor to live in a godly manner?

20. How do they affect your relationship with God?

Optional Exercise — Input from Friends and Family

To support your self-evaluation, we suggest you have one or more conversations with family members or close friends about the four charts on the previous pages. After you have completed your own answers to questions 1 through 20, set up a time to talk with someone who knows you well. Share your answers and ask for feedback about this exercise. On this page, record notes from the conversation. After the conversation, review your initial evaluation and make additional notes or changes.

Extraverts/Introverts

Sensors/Intuitives

Thinkers/Feelers

Judgers/Perceivers

Spiritual Discipline Exercise — Confession

Examining temperament can often reveal ways you have failed to demonstrate Christ's love to others. Take time now to pray and confess your sin to God. Acknowledge to Him that you have sinned not only against another person but against His standard for your life.

It's important to also experience His grace, because if you are a believer, Christ has paid for your sin on the cross. However, confession does not end with your communication with God. Go to the person you have wronged, acknowledge the sin to him or her, and ask for forgiveness. If there is any restitution to be made, do so as well. Zacchaeus provides us with a tremendous example of how you can pursue more than just a simple "I forgive you" from someone whom you have wronged (see Luke 19:1-10). You ought to seek to restore what was taken by your sin. Obviously, this may require some creativity on your part for a sin that does not involve material possessions being taken.

Write down the names of anyone with whom you have been prompted by God to seek forgiveness and reconciliation.

Heritage

1. Fill in the information about your birth.

   Date of birth:

   Place of birth:

   Parents:

   Siblings:

2. The rest of this section will help you examine your heritage as it has developed since your birth. In the spaces on page 111, record general facts about your heritage. (Don't describe specific past events or relationships—you'll do that later when you go through the *Community* study.) The definitions of mainstream culture, family culture, and subcultures on pages 45-47 will help you decide which box each of your heritage facts belongs in. The following lists might help you get the process started, but feel free to include other issues as well.

Functional Styles:

- Interpersonal communication (straightforward versus indirect, impersonal versus intimate, rational versus emotional)
- Household management (who performs chores, cooking, and maintenance; how much orderliness is valued)
- Expression of affection (verbal versus physical versus no expression at all)

- Conflict management (rare but explosive confrontations versus regular but calm confrontations or a complete lack of confrontations)
- Time (punctuality and its degree of importance)
- Money (spending habits and the priority of spending, saving, and giving)
- Recreational patterns (value of and involvement with physical exercise, outdoor activities, and social events)

Understanding of Success:

- View of competition and ambition
- Acceptable vocational goals
- Value of education
- Significance of family and personal reputation

Ethnicity and Its Implications:

- Ethnic environment (ethnically homogeneous versus multicultural versus minority in majority culture)
- View of other ethnic groups

Significance of Traditions:

- Celebrations and festivals
- Holidays
- Sports
- Arts (drama, music, visual art)

Mainstream Culture

Family Culture

Subcultures

Values I

Having made observations about various aspects of earthly identity, you will now turn to your values. Values are subjective judgments upon which you make decisions, use your time, and relate with people.

List what you consider to be your twelve most deeply held values. Typically these values stem from your earthly identity or are held in reaction to your earthly identity. Keep your observations from the exercises on gender, temperament, and heritage in mind as you identify what you consider to be your most deeply held values.

It's important to note that you may appear to have different values in different contexts. At work you may value efficiency to the extent that you will sacrifice relaxation, but on vacation you may value relaxation to the extent that you will sacrifice efficiency. This inventory is meant to determine which values you hold regardless of context. Those are your core values.

Here are some sample values. This list is not comprehensive and is meant only to spark your observations. Use additional ideas freely.

Peace: maintaining a sense of harmony and unity

Faith: depending on God

Grace: giving freely to others

Forgiveness: not holding grudges

Honesty: speaking truthfully

Confession: verbally admitting failures

Conforming: fitting in with a group or culture

Working alone: accomplishing tasks individually

Influencing: changing the way others live

Recognition: receiving feedback and approval for one's work

Accountability: being responsible to one another

Diversity of personality: valuing the uniqueness of yourself and others

Conflict resolution: getting conflicts out on the table

Shared goals: holding common goals along with others

Direction: having clear goals

Development: improving and refining skills and gifts

Inclusion: being included with others

Exclusion: being left alone

Intimacy: engaging deeply with others

Creativity: trying new things, expressing new thoughts, doing things differently

Training: repeatedly teaching effective principles/lessons/processes

Loyalty: sacrificing personal interests for those of others

Efficiency: pursuing high levels of productivity

Courtesy: having a friendly and hospitable attitude

Authenticity: expressing thoughts and emotions genuinely

Closure: completing tasks

Structure: having clearly defined expectations and plans

Spontaneity: continuously developing plans

My top twelve values (in no particular order):

1.   7.

2.   8.

3.   9.

4.   10.

5.   11.

6.   12.

Values II

Now that you have described what you understand to be your values, you will try to validate them. Transcribe your twelve most strongly held values to the table in this section. Analyze each value by providing specific examples from your life that confirm it.

For values you are able to back up, write "real" in the appropriate space. Write "ideal" if you can't think of any examples of how you live that value or if your examples are not generally characteristic of your life. Ideal values are those you attach importance to in your head but can't yet say are reflected in your life.

Value	Examples That Confirm It	Real or Ideal?
1.		
2.		
3.		
4.		

Value	Examples That Confirm It	Real or Ideal?
5.		
6.		
7.		
8.		
9.		
10.		
11.		
12.		

Identity in Christ

Biblical Statements

Take some time to read the following list of characteristics and their corresponding verses. Meditate on the verses as you read them. Place a check beside the characteristics and verses that you best understand and a minus beside the ones you least understand. Circle the statements that are the most meaningful to you.

Fellow heir with Christ (Romans 8:17; Galatians 4:7)

Justified (Romans 5:1)

Friend of Christ (John 15:15)

Citizen of heaven (Philippians 3:20)

Temple of God (1 Corinthians 3:16; 6:19)

Ambassador for Christ (2 Corinthians 5:20)

Coworker of God (1 Corinthians 3:9)

Saint (1 Corinthians 1:2; Ephesians 1:1; Philippians 1:1; Colossians 1:2)

One spirit with Christ (1 Corinthians 6:17)

One with the Father and Son (John 17:11,21-22)

New creature (2 Corinthians 5:17)

Righteousness of God (2 Corinthians 5:21)

One with all believers (Galatians 3:28)

Free (Galatians 5:1)

Blessed with every spiritual blessing (Ephesians 1:3)

Chosen, holy, and blameless before God (Ephesians 1:4)

Loved and chosen (1 Thessalonians 1:4)

Redeemed (Ephesians 1:7)

Forgiven (Ephesians 1:7)

Sealed with the Holy Spirit (Ephesians 1:13)

Alive with Christ (Ephesians 2:5)

God's workmanship (Ephesians 2:10)

Complete in Christ (Colossians 2:10)

Raised with Christ (Colossians 3:1)

Christ is life (Galatians 2:20; Colossians 3:4)

Child of God (John 1:12; Romans 8:15-17; Galatians 4:7; Ephesians 1:5)

Spiritual Discipline Exercise — Worship

Spend some time in worship this week. Set aside time to focus on the character of God rather than on your current circumstances, the tasks on your schedule, or your personal relationships. Express your appreciation for His work of bringing you into a reconciled relationship with Him, in which you have been made His adopted child.

Spiritual Gifts

Every member in a Christian community should become a minister to others' lives in some capacity. Spiritual giftedness describes the uniqueness of a person's design as a minister in the body of Christ. This exercise is designed to help you make observations about your spiritual giftedness.

1. Read each of the following passages. Write what each passage teaches you about spiritual gifts.

   Romans 12:1-8

   1 Corinthians 12:1-31

2. The best way to discover your gifts is to experiment. Ministry involves formal or informal ways of serving. For instance, you may regularly take food to those in need, or you may typically contribute money (beyond your regular tithing) for church projects. If you have not had any experience in ministry or service, simply ask a church staff member or elder how you can help, and just start serving. Or look around you for something that needs to be done for others, and start doing it. Finally, small

groups offer many opportunities to serve. You might be able to assist your group leader with some task, such as coordinating refreshments for the meetings or gathering and following up on prayer requests.

If you have already been serving, consider how you can improve your service. Make a point this week of getting involved in some area of service. What have you chosen?

3. Assess your gift(s) in relation to the Bible passages in question 1, counsel with other believers, and past experience. To aid in that process, write answers to the following questions. If you have limited experience in ministry, simply write as much as you can, keeping unanswered questions in the back of your mind to consider after you have gained some firsthand ministry experience.

   • What aspects of ministry do you enjoy doing? (Some examples are teaching a third-grade Sunday school class, participating in evangelistic outreach programs, providing refreshments for small-group meetings, checking in with group members who have missed meetings, and praying for others.)

- What aspects of ministry do others enjoy or benefit from when you are doing them?

- What aspects of ministry have others in the community affirmed in you? (You can add answers to this question after your group meets to discuss gifts.)

- When you look at the church today, what do you see as the church's greatest need?

- What aspects of ministry do you know you're *not* gifted in?

If you have further questions about gifts, ask your small-group leader or your pastor. Churches vary in their understanding of spiritual gifts, so we have deliberately avoided defining gifts in a particular way. Your pastor can help you do that.

Leader's Guide

Introduction

This leader's guide will:
- Explain the intended purpose of each session and how each session fits into the entire study
- Provide you with plenty of discussion questions so that you can choose a few that suit your group
- Suggest other ways of interacting over the material

The first step in leading this study is to read "A Model of Spiritual Transformation" beginning on page 9. The section describes three broad approaches to growth and explains how the four studies in the series fit together.

There's more involved in leading a small group, however, than just understanding the study and its objective. The main skill you'll need is creating a group environment that facilitates authentic interaction among people. Every leader does this in his or her own style, but here are two principles necessary for all:

1. *Avoid the temptation to speak whenever people don't immediately respond to one of your questions.* As the leader, you may feel pressure to break the silence. Often, though, leaders overestimate how much silence has gone by. Several seconds of silence may seem like a minute to the leader. However, usually people just need time to collect their thoughts before they respond. If you wait patiently for their responses, they will usually take that to mean you really do want them to say what they think. On the other hand, if you consistently break the silence yourself, they may not feel the need to speak up.

2. *Avoid being a problem solver.* If you immediately try to solve every problem that group members voice, they won't feel comfortable sharing issues of personal struggle. Why? Because most people, when sharing their problems, initially want to receive acceptance and empathy rather than advice. They want others to understand and care about the troubled state of their soul. Giving immediate advice can often communicate that you feel they are not bright enough to figure out the solution.

Getting a Small Group Started

You may be gathering a group of friends to do a study together or possibly you've volunteered to lead a group that your church is assembling. Regardless of the circumstances, God has identified you as the leader.

You are probably a peer of the other group members. Some may have read more theology than you, some may have more church ministry experience than you, and yet God has providentially chosen you as the leader. You're not the "teacher" or the sole possessor of wisdom—you are simply responsible to create an atmosphere that facilitates genuine interaction.

One of the most effective ways you can serve your group is to *make clear what is expected*. You are the person who informs group members. They need to know, for example, where and when your first meeting will be held. If you're meeting in a home and members need maps, make sure they receive them in a timely manner. If members don't have study books, help them each obtain one. To create a hospitable setting for your meetings, you will need to plan for refreshments or delegate that responsibility to others. A group phone and e-mail list may also be helpful; ask the group if it's okay to distribute their contact information to one another. Make sure there's a sense of order. You may even want to chart out a tentative schedule of all the sessions, including any off weeks for holidays.

The first several sessions are particularly important because they are when you will communicate your vision for the group. You'll want to explain your vision several times during your first several meetings. Many people need to hear it several times before it really sinks in, and some will probably miss the first meeting or two. Communicate your vision and expectations concisely so that plenty of time remains for group discussion. People will drop out if the first session feels like a monologue from the leader.

At your first meeting, it is valuable to let group members each tell a brief history of themselves. This could involve a handful of facts about themselves and how they ended up in the group. Also, in your first or second meeting, ask group members to share their expectations. The discussion may take the greater part of a meeting, but it's worth the time invested because it will help you understand each person's perspective. Here are some questions for initiating a discussion of group members' expectations:

- How well do you expect to get to know others in the group?
- Describe your previous experiences with small groups. Do you expect this group to be similar or different?
- What do you hope the group will be like by the time our study ends?
- How do you think this group will contribute to your walk with Christ?
- Do you need to finish the meeting by a certain time, or do you prefer open-ended meetings? Do you expect to complete this study in ten sessions, or will you be happy extending it by a few sessions if the additional time serves your other goals for the group?

If you give people more than a minute or two to share their personal histories and you have an extended discussion of people's expectations, you probably won't actually begin session 1 in this study guide until the second or third time you meet. This is more likely if your group is just forming than if your group has been together for some time. By the time you start the first session in the study guide, group members ought to be accustomed to interacting with one another. This early investment will pay big dividends. If you plan to take a whole meeting (or even two) to lay this kind of groundwork, be sure to tell the group what you're doing and why. Otherwise, some people may think you're simply inefficient and unable to keep the group moving forward.

Remember that many people will feel nervous during the first meeting. This is natural; don't feel threatened by it. Your attitude and demeanor will set the tone. If you are passive, the group will lack direction and vision. If you are all business and no play, they will expect that the group will have a formal atmosphere, and you will struggle to get people to lighten up. If you are all play and no business, they will expect the group to be all fluff and won't take it seriously. Allow the group some time and freedom to form a "personality." If many group members enjoy a certain activity, join in with them. Don't try to conform the group to your interests. You may have to be willing to explore new activities.

What does the group need from you initially as the leader?

- *Approachability:* Be friendly, ask questions, avoid dominating the discussion, engage with group members before and after the sessions, allow group members opportunities to ask you questions too.

- *Connections:* Pay attention to how you can facilitate bonding. (For example, if you learn in separate conversations that two group members went to State University, you might say, "Joe, did you know that Tom also went to State U?")

- *Communication of Logistics:* Be simple, clear, and concise. (For instance, be clear about what will be involved in the group sessions, how long they will last, and where and when they will occur.)

- *Summary of Your Leadership Style:* You might want to put together some thoughts about your style of leadership and be prepared to share them with the group. You might include such issues as:

    1. The degree of flexibility with which you operate (for example, your willingness to go on "rabbit trails" versus staying on topic)

    2. Your level of commitment to having prayer or worship as a part of the group

    3. Your attentiveness, or lack thereof, to logistics (making sure to discuss the details surrounding your group, such as when and where you are meeting, or how to maintain communication with one another if something comes up)

    4. The degree to which you wear your emotions on your sleeve

    5. Any aspects of your personality that have often been misunderstood (for instance, "People sometimes think that I'm not interested in what they are saying because I don't immediately respond, when really I'm just pondering what they were saying.")

6. Any weaknesses you are aware of as a leader (for example, "Because I can tend to dominate the group by talking too much, I will appreciate anybody letting me know if I am doing so." Or, "I get very engaged in discussion and can consequently lose track of time, so I may need you to help me keep on task so we finish on time.")

7. How you plan to address any concerns you have with group members (for instance, "If I have concerns about the way anyone is interacting in the group, perhaps by consistently offending another group member, I will set up time to get together and address it with that person face-to-face.")

- *People Development:* Allow group members to exercise their spiritual gifts. See their development not as a threat to your leadership but as a sign of your success as a leader. For instance, if group members enjoy worshiping together and you have someone who can lead the group in worship, encourage that person to do so. However, give direction in this so that the person knows exactly what you expect. Make sure he or she understands how much worship time you want.

Beginning the Sessions

Before you jump into session 1, make sure that group members have had a chance to read "A Model of Spiritual Transformation" beginning on page 9 and "A Method for the Biblical Exercises" beginning on page 17. Also, ask if they have done what is listed in the "Preparation" section of session 1. Emphasize that the assignments for each session are as important as the group meetings and that inadequate preparation for a session diminishes the whole group's experience.

Overview of *Identity*

In *Identity*, we often refer to "earthly identity" and "heavenly identity." Earthly identity refers to those aspects of a person that both believers and unbelievers have: roles, gender, temperament, and heritage. The components of earthly identity are addressed in sessions 2 through 5. In those sessions, we ask, "How do your views of your roles, gender, temperament, and heritage affect your attempts to love God and others?"

Heavenly identity signifies those aspects of a person that only believers have, such as the impact of Christ on our values, our position in Christ, and our spiritual gifts. These are addressed in sessions 6 through 10.

The Order of Sessions

We address earthly identity first, make a transition by discussing personal values, and then discuss heavenly identity. We want group members to see themselves stripped of Christ and then see how being in Christ has transformed their identity. Thus, the question becomes, "What areas of my identity need transformation, and what areas are part of my unique personality that God can use for His glory?"

Life Inventory

"Life Inventory" helps group members identify general characteristics of their lives. Most sessions have a corresponding "Life Inventory" section. Group members do the "Life Inventory" exercises individually, outside the group meetings. You as the leader also need to complete the corresponding "Life Inventory" section before each session. Doing so not only will benefit you personally but will help you think of some of your own discussion questions.

Discussion Questions

This "Leader's Guide" contains questions that we think will help you attain the goal of each session and build community in your group. Use our discussion questions in addition to the ones you come up with on your own, but don't feel pressured to use all of them. However, we think it's wise to use some of them. If one question is not a good vehicle for discussion, then use another. It can be helpful to rephrase the questions in your own words.

Session 1: Human Nature

In this first session, you don't want to get bogged down in a discussion of creationism versus evolutionism. Rather, you want to guide the discussion toward the most fundamental aspects of human nature as designed by God.

The chapters in Genesis are central to this discussion. To some degree, your discussion will revolve around biblical concepts rather than personal issues of faith. You may need to keep this session from being too abstract if you have a group that likes abstract discussion. Make sure you spend a significant amount of time addressing the more personal questions, which are toward the end of the list of suggested questions.

Because group members should have done a personal Bible study in Genesis in preparation for this session, you might want to plan some time for them to share what they found in their personal study. Limit this time so you have time for wider discussion as well.

You may have group members who have no experience in personal Bible study. Try to discern sensitively whether any group member feels ashamed about a lack of biblical literacy and Bible study skills. Affirm everyone, even if they're new to the Bible. They probably have other gifts that your group will need just as much. Part of your job is to uncover and help the group value those gifts. Offer help to anyone who wants coaching in Bible study. The following are suggested discussion questions:

1. How might the secular world describe what is fundamentally true of human beings?

2. How should we as Christians respond to the various views of human nature in the secular world?

3. Why do we trust the account of Genesis instead of our own abilities to make sense of our purpose?

4. From your study of Genesis, what strikes you in a new way about human nature?

5. How does this view of human nature affect the way you understand yourself?

6. How does this view change the way you think about your work? How might you reflect God's nature in your workplace?

7. How does this view of human nature affect the way you think about your home life?

8. How does this view affect the way you think about, interact with, and serve other people (both believers and unbelievers)?

9. How can our distinctive view of human nature make us, as believers, a light in the unbelieving world?

Session 2: Roles

We express our identity (who we are) in how we do what we do. Consider 1 John 2:9: "Anyone who claims to be in the light but hates his brother is still in the darkness." Our attitudes and the condition of our soul will ultimately surface in our behavior. Jesus says, "But the things that come out of the mouth come from the heart, and these make a man 'unclean'" (Matthew 15:18). How you perform your roles is an expression of who you are.

The main purpose of this session is to help group members clearly see that what they do is not what defines them. Direct group members toward reflection about who they are, not what tasks they do.

People's answers to the questions in this section will give you a good feel of where they stand on the issue of self-examination. Some people resist personal evaluation; they aren't eager to look inside themselves or reflect on how they do what they do. Because this study leads members through many exercises of self-evaluation, a willingness to examine oneself is an important characteristic to look for in group members. If you observe resistance, you may want to initiate a conversation with the person to ask what he or she thinks of the study and its encouragement of personal evaluation.

1. What's at stake if we don't examine our lives?

   (Sample answers)
   • We don't learn how to develop more loving responses to others.
   • We don't have our faith in Christ reinforced by remembering how He has sustained and guided us in the past.

• We don't realize our blind spots.

• We don't develop confidence in what our gifts are with which we can serve the body.

2. What do you think Proverbs 14:8 means? (The point is most likely that those who don't evaluate themselves can be easily deceived about themselves. This self-deception is a kind of foolishness.) Can you think of how a lack of self-understanding can lead to foolishness?

Turn to the "Life Inventory: Roles" exercise beginning on page 91. Use the information you wrote on the chart as you answer the following five questions:

1. How would you identify yourself without using the roles you listed on your chart?

2. Is there anything listed as a role on your chart that you feel you must include to accurately identify yourself? Why?

3. Consider a time when you transitioned out of a role that you considered significant. How did the loss of this role change the way that you viewed yourself?

4. What are some distinctions between roles and identity?

5. What aspects of your identity remain consistent in spite of changes in roles?

Session 3: Gender

The goal of this session is not to answer all the debates in the Christian community about women and their role in the church or society. Rather, the objective is simply for group members to think about how they view masculinity and femininity. Encourage them to consider how that view developed in their life. Remind the group that much of this study is concerned with making observations about their own sense of identity. Their understanding of gender is a significant part of how they view themselves.

As you begin, read aloud the definitions of gender and sex from pages 33-37. Make sure your group members understand the distinction between the two.

The following discussion questions ought to connect well with the "Life Inventory" exercise on gender. Rather than having everyone share answers to each of the fifteen questions in the "Life Inventory" exercise, let your discussion questions bring out the most significant aspects of each person's exercise. That will produce a more interesting discussion.

1. Give three statements about what it means for you to be a man/woman.

2. Where or from whom did you learn those things?

3. How have sexuality and gender been blurred in our contemporary society?

4. Who taught you or modeled for you what it means to be a man or woman?

5. In what ways was it a healthy model, and in what ways was it not?

6. In your opinion, what happens to people who have distorted views of their gender?

Optional questions for married couples' groups:

1. What does it mean for you to be a husband/father or wife/mother?

2. Do you have specific views of gender that affect the way you and your spouse fulfill your roles within your household? If so, describe those views.

3. How did you develop these views?

Optional questions for men's or women's groups:

1. How does your sexuality affect the way you perceive yourself in the workplace? At home?

2. How comfortable are you working with people of the opposite sex? Do you have different expectations of them? If so, how did those different expectations develop in your life?

Session 4: Temperament

This is another session in which you need to be sensitive to group members. Some people will resist temperament assessment exercises. The process frustrates others. Continue to emphasize that this is a time of observation, not judgment. Ask group members to observe not just what categories of temperament they fall into but also how those characteristics affect their relationships with God and others.

Avoid a dry sharing time where everyone goes around the room and shares results of their temperament exercise. Instead, draw out people's results through the discussion by using the following questions:

1. What from the charts in the "Life Inventory" exercise would you say are the most accurate statements about your temperament?

2. Where in your roles of life (family, jobs, ministries) do you see the impact of your temperament? In what ways?

3. What challenges in loving God and people do you face as a result of your temperament? What hinders you in your relationships?

4. What aspects of your temperament help you love people well?

5. How does your temperament affect the way you relate to God?

6. As members of the body of Christ, how should we approach temperament differently from the way the world does?

It's essential that before session 5, group members complete both the "Heritage" exercise and the "Values I" exercise in "Life Inventory." Why? Because in session 6 they will go back to the values they identified in "Values I" and try to "validate" them (that is, see how those values play out in their life). It's important for them to identify their values *before* they know they'll be asked to validate them. If they do both "Values I" and "Values II" at the same time, it will be hard to resist "cheating," and they'll lose the benefit of the exercise. It's not necessary that they understand this rationale; it's only necessary that they do "Values I" before session 5 and then "Values II" before session 6.

Session 5: Heritage

You will continue to make observations about yourselves in this session. The content paragraphs that define mainstream culture, family culture, and subcultures are meant to clarify the terms you'll use in your discussion.

Because group members will have read the session and completed the "Life Inventory: Heritage" exercise, you may want to start the discussion with the following questions:

1. What was the most surprising thing you observed about your heritage?

2. What did you observe that you have never considered about your heritage before?

Or you can begin the session by asking what the group members think about the Hesselgrave quote that appears in the "Content" section. It will be important to note if group members downplay the significance of heritage. Wherever they stand on the issue, you want to help them understand the importance of heritage.

Be especially sensitive and careful to listen in this session. People may share experiences with racism, abusive backgrounds, or other severely painful events. This session can begin the process of opening up difficult issues from their pasts.

You can spend this meeting letting each person summarize his or her notes from the "Life Inventory: Heritage" exercise. Emphasize that there isn't time for everyone to share everything they wrote down. People should share a few generalizations and implications of their heritage. Ask group members to read through what they have written about their birth (page 109) and then to give a few highlights from their mainstream culture, family culture, and subcultures entries. Give each person about ten minutes to share—if you have five people, this will use up a ninety-minute meeting. (It may help to assign a timekeeper, as some people like to talk about their pasts.)

If people in your group claim that their heritage has little to no effect on the way they live out their roles, this will be a signal to sensitively probe. Regardless of our attempts to be neutral to our heritage, it significantly affects the way we live. As a leader, you want to surface that reality. While it's true that we need to turn from many influences of our heritage in order to pursue godly living, we are trying to postpone that conversation for a few more sessions and focus now on the real impact of heritage.

The following questions are an alternative to letting each group member summarize his or her findings. This is especially helpful if you have a large group of six or more, because sharing a summary of findings will take a great deal of time. Not everyone needs to answer each question.

1. What characteristic from your mainstream culture influenced you the most?

2. What was the most dominant characteristic of your family culture? How has it influenced your view of yourself or others?

3. What characteristic from your subcultures influenced you the most?

4. What challenges in loving God and people do you face as a result of your heritage? What advantages does it give?

5. How has your heritage positively affected your roles in life? What about negative effects?

6. What about your heritage do you embrace? What do you reject? Why?

Time Alone with God

After session 5, you have two options. You can cancel your group time for a week and encourage group members to take some time, perhaps an hour or more, alone with God. This is the suggested option. It will provide them with an opportunity to reflect upon their "Values" exercises in a time of prayer. However, you may feel that you need to press on to session 6 directly.

Session 6: Values

This session is the transition from earthly identity to heavenly identity. Our values are the channel through which our earthly identity profoundly influences our lives, and our values are the channel through which Christ transforms us. Try to help group members make a connection between their earthly identity and the values they hold or the values they have rejected.

If your group did the optional "Time Alone with God" exercise, you may open the discussion with questions 1 and 2. If your group did not do the "Time Alone with God" exercise, begin with question 3.

1. Did you spend time alone with God?

2. How was it?

3. How has your earthly identity (gender, temperament, and heritage) influenced the list of twelve values you recorded in your values exercises? In other words, where did your values come from?

4. Have you intentionally rejected values from your heritage? If so, why?

5. Going back to the "Values II" exercise beginning on page 114, which values were evident in your life (real values)? Explain.

6. What are some principles you can derive from your real values?

7. Which values were not evident in your life (ideal values)? Why do you think you initially stated each as a value you hold?

8. What keeps those ideal values from being real?

9. Should all believers have the same set of values? Why, or why not?

10. What one ideal value are you committing to making real in your life? How do you intend to do so?

Session 7: Identity in Christ

In this session, you will barely scratch the surface of the topic of identity in Christ. However, if group members go through the session's corresponding "Life Inventory" exercise diligently, they will discover a wealth of knowledge about their identity in Christ. Your group discussion will center on how hard it is to reconcile the reality of our identity in Christ with our perception of our current life, which is so greatly influenced by our earthly identity.

1. Which characteristics from the list do you best understand?

2. Which do you least understand?

3. Which characteristics do you identify with most?

4. Which do you identify with least?

5. Read Romans 6:1-11. What emphasis does Paul place upon knowing this information?

6. Do you think just knowing who we are in Christ will help us in our struggle against sin? How, or why not?

7. Do you think a change in identity will produce a change in lifestyle? Why, or why not?

8. What characteristics besides love come to mind when you think of your identity in Christ?

9. What characteristics besides love might nonbelievers think of in regards to Christians?

10. What ought to be the priority of love in comparison with other characteristics in our lives as Christians?

11. How does the priority of love reveal Christ and glorify Christ to others?

12. How would you expect nonbelievers in your community to respond if Christians were primarily characterized by love?

Session 8: Saint or Sinner

We're careful not to claim that the Christian's identity is characterized solely by sin nor solely by righteousness. We can't ignore the struggle we encounter with sin, yet we have been redeemed from the dominion of sin.

As we've seen in past sessions, our personal heritage (mainstream culture, family culture, subcultures) affects our behavior and the way we view ourselves.

1. If we think of our new status as a heavenly heritage, how will that heritage affect the way we view ourselves and behave? How do we integrate the two heritages?

2. What does it mean that we are no longer under the dominion or control of sin?

3. Why do we sometimes feel enslaved to certain sins if we're no longer under sin's dominion?

4. Why don't we feel more ruled by the kingdom of righteousness?

5. How can nonbelievers do good deeds and believers do bad deeds when neither situation truly reflects the kingdom that rules them?

Session 9: Spiritual Gifts

This session is not meant to be merely a spiritual gifts assessment test. Rather, it's designed for group members to evaluate themselves and, more important, to receive feedback from others concerning their spiritual gifts.

1. Think of a time when you felt a strong sense that God was using you personally, whether in the life of another person or in a community endeavor. Perhaps it was something you didn't initially pay much attention to, but someone else told you how much he or she appreciated your service. Describe your perception of how God used you.

2. Briefly share with the group any spiritual gifts that you identified in the "Life Inventory: Spiritual Gifts" exercise. Give examples from your life that demonstrate these gifts.

3. What one gift do you want to commit to exercising or focus on developing? How will you do so?

Have the group share what they think each person's spiritual gifts are. You may want to emphasize that this process is not conclusive. Members may receive feedback that identifies their giftedness inaccurately. However, the process of receiving affirmation from a community about each other's gifts is important. The more experience your group has with one another, the more accurate and powerful the affirmation and encouragement will be.

You will notice that the content covered in this session is very limited. This is because church bodies hold various views on spiritual gifts. For this session, you can focus on the experience of group members receiving affirmation from each other. However, if you desire to include more content about spiritual gifts and the definitions of particular gifts, consult with your church leadership about what resources they recommend.

Session 10: Corporate Aspects of Identity in Christ

This session is designed with two things in mind. First, it's the finale of the study. Far too many people try to build a completely individual sense of Christian identity. There is no such thing found in Scripture. Corporate aspects are central, so it makes sense that you'd discuss them in your final meeting.

Second, this session provides a natural transition into the *Community* study if your group chooses to continue in this series. That study will go into detail about components necessary for authentic Christian community as well as guide the group through exercises that foster the growth of genuine community.

1. Was the idea of "the new man" as community a new discovery for you? If so, is it hard to accept? What implications does this have on your identity?

2. How does this idea affect the way you understand growth in the Christian life?

3. How does this view change the value you place on being part of Christian community?

Make sure that your group has a chance to interact on one of the following questions to wrap up the topic of identity and reflect on what they've learned.

1. What in this study has affected you most concerning your identity?

2. How will this affect your future? Your perspective in life? Your motivation for ministering to and serving others? Your commitment to being an ambassador for Christ in the world?

Conclusion

We hope this study has been helpful for you and your group members. We are committed to providing materials that help believers grow in Christ through small-group communities. Don't hesitate to contact us if you have questions!

Phone: (214) 841-3515
E-mail: sf@dts.edu

Notes

A Method for the Biblical Exercises

1. Howard G. Hendricks and William D. Hendricks, *Living By the Book* (Chicago: Moody, 1991), p. 166.

Session 3: Gender

1. Raymond C. Ortlund Jr., "Male-Female Equality and Male Headship: Genesis 1–3," in *Recovering Biblical Manhood and Womanhood: A Response to Evangelical Feminism*, ed. John Piper and Wayne Grudem (Wheaton, Ill.: Crossway, 1991), p. 97.
2. Ortlund, p. 97.
3. Allen P. Ross, *Creation and Blessing: A Guide to the Study and Exposition of Genesis* (Grand Rapids, Mich.: Baker, 1988), p. 126.
4. Ross, p. 126.
5. Ortlund, p. 99.
6. Ross, p. 147.

Session 5: Heritage

1. "heritage," *Webster's Encyclopedic Unabridged Dictionary of the English Language* (New York: Gramercy Books, 1996), p. 664.
2. David J. Hesselgrave, "Christ and Culture," in *Perspectives on the World Christian Movement: A Reader* (Pasadena, Calif.: William Carey Library, 1981), p. 366.
3. Louis J. Luzbetak, *The Church and Cultures: New Perspectives in Missiological Anthropology* (Maryknoll, N.Y.: Orbis Books, 1988), pp. 198-199.

Session 6: Values

1. "value," *Merriam-Webster's Collegiate Dictionary*, 11th ed. (Springfield, Mass.: Merriam-Webster, 2003), p. 1382.

Session 9: Spiritual Gifts

1. J. I. Packer, *Keep in Step with the Spirit* (Grand Rapids, Mich.: Fleming H. Revell, 1994), p. 82.
2. Packer, p. 83.

Session 10: Corporate Aspects of Identity in Christ

1. Darrell L. Bock, "'The New Man' As Community in Colossians and Ephesians," in *Integrity of Heart, Skillfulness of Hands*, ed. Charles H. Dyer and Roy B. Zuck (Grand Rapids, Mich.: Baker, 1994), p. 157.
2. Bock, p. 159.

Life Inventory

1. David Keirsey and Marilyn Bates, *Please Understand Me: Character and Temperament Types* (Del Mar, Calif.: Prometheus Nemesis Book Company, 1984), pp. 14-26.
2. Paul D. Tieger and Barbara Barron-Tieger, *Do What You Are: Discover the Perfect Career for You Through the Secrets of Personality Type*, 2nd ed. (Boston: Little, Brown, 1995), p. 13.
3. Keirsey and Bates, p. 15.

OTHER BOOKS IN THE TRANSFORMING LIFE SERIES.

Community

Explore what it takes to combat isolation and build true Christian community.
1-57683-559-6

Integrity

Identify ways to overcome the habits that are contrary to the values you profess as a Christian. Instead discover Christlike character traits you can develop and live out.
1-57683-561-8

Ministry

Your interests, struggles, and talents can help you discern how God has uniquely designed you to serve. This study will help you find your unique niche in the body of Christ.
1-57683-562-6

To get your copies, visit your local bookstore, call 1-800-366-7788, or log on to www.navpress.com. Ask for a FREE catalog of NavPress products. Offer BPA.